CW00401706

CIMA

## How to access your on-line resources

Kaplan Financial students will have a MyKaplan account and these extra resources will be available to you online. You do not need to register again, as this process was completed when you enrolled. If you are having problems accessing online materials, please ask your course administrator.

If you are not studying with Kaplan and did not purchase your book via a Kaplan website, to unlock your extra online resources please go to www.en-gage.co.uk (even if you have set up an account and registered books previously). You will then need to enter the ISBN number (on the title page and back cover) and the unique pass key number contained in the scratch panel below to gain access.

You will also be required to enter additional information during this process to set up or confirm your account details.

If you purchased via the Kaplan Publishing website you will automatically receive an e-mail invitation to register your details and gain access to your content. If you do not receive the e-mail or book content, please contact Kaplan Publishing.

## Your code and information

This code can only be used once for the registration of one book online. This registration and your online content will expire when the final sittings for the examinations covered by this book have taken place. Please allow one hour from the time you submit your book details for us to process your request.

Please scratch the film to access your unique code.

Please be aware that this code is case-sensitive and you will need to include the dashes within the passcode, but not when entering the ISBN.

KAPLAN

PUBLISHING

# Subject BA3

## Fundamentals of Financial Accounting

## EXAM PRACTICE KIT

**British Library Cataloguing-in-Publication Data**

A catalogue record for this book is available from the British Library.

**Published by: Kaplan Publishing UK**

Unit 2 The Business Centre, Molly Millars Lane, Wokingham, Berkshire RG41 2QZ

ISBN: 978-1-78740-492-2

© Kaplan Financial Limited, 2019

**Acknowledgements**

This Product includes propriety content of the International Accounting Standards Board which is overseen by the IFRS Foundation, and is used with the express permission of the IFRS Foundation under licence. All rights reserved. No part of this publication may be reproduced, stored in a retrieval system, or transmitted in any form or by any means, electronic, mechanical, photocopying, recording, or otherwise, without prior written permission of Kaplan Publishing and the IFRS Foundation.

The IFRS Foundation logo, the IASB logo, the IFRS for SMEs logo, the "Hexagon Device", "IFRS Foundation", "eIFRS", "IAS", "IASB", "IFRS for SMEs", "IFRS", "IASs", "IFRSs", "International Accounting Standards" and "International Financial Reporting Standards", "IFRIC" and "IFRS Taxonomy" are Trade Marks of the IFRS Foundation.

**Trade Marks**

The IFRS Foundation logo, the IASB logo, the IFRS for SMEs logo, the "Hexagon Device", "IFRS Foundation", "eIFRS", "IAS", "IASB", "IFRS for SMEs", "NIIF" IASs" "IFRS", "IFRSs", "International Accounting Standards", "International Financial Reporting Standards", "IFRIC", "SIC" and "IFRS Taxonomy".

Further details of the Trade Marks including details of countries where the Trade Marks are registered or applied for are available from the Foundation on request.

# CONTENTS

| | Page |
|---|---|
| Index to questions and answers | P.4 |
| Syllabus guidance, learning objectives and verbs | P.5 |
| Objective tests | P.9 |
| Syllabus outline – BA3 | P.11 |
| Learning outcomes and indicative syllabus content | P.13 |

## Section

| | | |
|---|---|---|
| 1 | Objective test questions | 1 |
| 2 | Answers to objective test questions | 51 |
| 3 | Practice assessment questions | 87 |
| 4 | Answers to practice assessment questions | 101 |
| 5 | References | 113 |

This document references IFRS® Standards and IAS® Standards, which are authored by the International Accounting Standards Board (the Board), and published in the 2019 IFRS Standards Red Book.

Quality and accuracy are of the utmost importance to us so if you spot an error in any of our products, please send an email to mykaplanreporting@kaplan.com with full details.

Our Quality Co-ordinator will work with our technical team to verify the error and take action to ensure it is corrected in future editions.

# INDEX TO QUESTIONS AND ANSWERS

## OBJECTIVE TEST QUESTIONS

# SYLLABUS GUIDANCE, LEARNING OBJECTIVES AND VERBS

## A THE CERTIFICATE IN BUSINESS ACCOUNTING (CERT BA)

The Cert BA provides a foundation in the essential elements of accounting and business. This includes the Fundamentals of Business Economics. There are four subject areas, which are all tested by computer-based assessment (CBA). The four subjects are:

- BA1: Fundamentals of Business Economics
- BA2: Fundamentals of Management Accounting
- BA3: Fundamentals of Financial Accounting
- BA4: Fundamentals of Ethics, Corporate Governance and Business Law

The Cert BA is both a qualification in its own right and an entry route to the next stage in CIMA's examination structure.

The examination structure after the Certificate comprises:

- Operational Level
- Managerial Level
- Strategic Level

The CIMA Qualification includes more advanced topics in Accounting and Business. It is therefore very important that you apply yourself to Fundamentals of Business Economics, not only because it is part of the Certificate, but also as a platform for more advanced studies. It is thus an important step in becoming a qualified member of the Chartered Institute of Management Accountants.

## B AIMS OF THE SYLLABUS

The aims of the syllabus are

- to provide for the Institute, together with the practical experience requirements, an adequate basis for assuring society that those admitted to membership are competent to act as management accountants for entities, whether in manufacturing, commercial or service organisations, in the public or private sectors of the economy;
- to enable the Institute to examine whether prospective members have an adequate knowledge, understanding and mastery of the stated body of knowledge and skills;
- to complement the Institute's practical experience and skills development requirements.

# C STUDY WEIGHTINGS

A percentage weighting is shown against each topic in the syllabus. This is intended as a guide to the proportion of study time each topic requires.

All topics in the syllabus must be studied, since any single examination question may examine more than one topic, or carry a higher proportion of marks than the percentage study time suggested.

The weightings do not specify the number of marks that will be allocated to topics in the examination.

# D CIMA'S HIERARCHY OF LEARNING OBJECTIVES

CIMA places great importance on the definition of verbs in structuring Objective Test Examinations. It is therefore crucial that you understand the verbs in order to appreciate the depth and breadth of a topic and the level of skill required. The CIMA Cert BA syllabus learning outcomes and objective test questions will focus on levels one, two and three of the CIMA's hierarchy of learning objectives (knowledge, comprehension and application). However, as you progress to the Operational, Management and Strategic levels of the CIMA Professional Qualification, testing will include levels four and five of the hierarchy. As you complete your CIMA Professional Qualification, you can therefore expect to be tested on knowledge, comprehension, application, analysis and evaluation.

In CIMA Cert BA Objective Test Examinations you will meet verbs from only levels 1, 2, and 3 of the hierarchy which are as follows:

| Skill level | Verbs used | Definition |
| --- | --- | --- |
| **Level 1**<br>**Knowledge**<br>What you are expected to know | List | Make a list of |
| | State | Express, fully or clearly, the details/facts of |
| | Define | Give the exact meaning of |
| | Outline | Give a summary of |

For example you could be asked to define economic terms such as 'inflation' (BA1), or to define the term 'management accounting' (BA2) or to state the accounting entries required to record the revaluation surplus arising on revaluation of land and buildings (BA3).

| Skill level | Verbs used | Definition |
| --- | --- | --- |
| **Level 2**<br>**Comprehension**<br>What you are expected to understand | Describe | Communicate the key features of |
| | Distinguish | Highlight the differences between |
| | Explain | Make clear or intelligible/state the meaning or purpose of |
| | Identify | Recognise, establish or select after consideration |
| | Illustrate | Use an example to describe or explain something |

For example you could be asked to explain the components of the circular flow of funds (BA1), or distinguish between financial accounting and management accounting (BA3) or distinguish between express terms and implied terms of a contract of employment (BA4).

| Skill level | Verbs used | Definition |
|---|---|---|
| **Level 3**<br>**Application**<br>How you are expected to apply your knowledge | Apply | Put to practical use |
| | Calculate | Ascertain or reckon mathematically |
| | Conduct | Organise and carry out |
| | Demonstrate | Prove with certainty or exhibit by practical means |
| | Prepare | Make or get ready for use |
| | Reconcile | Make or prove consistent/compatible |

For example you could be asked to reconcile the differences between profits calculated using absorption costing and marginal costing (BA2), or to calculate the gain or loss on disposal of a noncurrent asset (BA3) or to apply relevant principles to determine the outcome of a law-based or ethical problem (BA4).

For reference, levels 4 and 5 of the hierarchy require demonstration of analysis and evaluation skills respectively. Further detail on levels 4 and 5 of the hierarchy which are tested in the CIMA Professional Qualification can be obtained from the CIMA website, www.cimaglobal.com.

# OBJECTIVE TESTS

Objective Test questions require you to choose or provide a response to a question whose correct answer is predetermined.

The most common types of Objective Test question you will see are:

- **multiple choice**, where you have to choose the correct answer(s) from a list of possible answers – this could either be numbers or text.

- **multiple response** with more choices and answers, for example, choosing two correct answers from a list of five available answers – this could either be numbers or text.

- **number entry**, where you give your numeric answer to one or more parts of a question, for example, gross profit is $25,000 and the accrual for heat and light charges is $750.

- **drag and drop**, where you match one or more items with others from the list available, for example, matching several accounting terms with the appropriate definition

- **drop down**, where you choose the correct answer from those available in a drop down menu, for example, choosing the correct calculation of an accounting ratio, or stating whether an individual statement is true or false. This can also be included with a number entry style question.

- **hot spot**, where, for example, you use your computer cursor or mouse to identify the point of profit maximisation on a graph

CIMA has provided the following guidance relating to the format of questions and their marking:

- questions which require narrative responses to be typed will not be used

- for number entry questions, clear guidance will usually be given about the format in which the answer is required e.g. 'to the nearest $' or 'to two decimal places'.

- item set questions provide a scenario which then forms the basis of more than one question (usually 2 and 4 questions). These sets of questions would appear together in the test and are most likely to appear in BA2 and BA3

- all questions are independent so that, where questions are based on a common item set scenario, each question will be distinct and the answer to a later question will not be dependent upon answering an earlier question correctly

- all items are equally weighted and, where a question consists of more than one element, all elements must be answered correctly for the question to be marked correct.

Throughout this Exam Practice Kit we have introduced these types of questions, but obviously we have had to label answers A, B, C etc. rather than using click boxes. For convenience we have retained quite a few questions where an initial scenario leads to a number of sub-questions. There will be questions of this type in the Objective Test Examination but they will rarely have more than three sub-questions.

## Guidance re CIMA on-screen calculator

As part of the CIMA Objective Test software, candidates are provided with a calculator. This calculator is on-screen and is available for the duration of the assessment. The calculator is available in Objective Test Examinations for BA1, BA2 and BA3 (it is not required for BA4).

Guidance regarding calculator use in the Objective Test Examinations is available online at: https://connect.cimaglobal.com/

## CIMA Cert BA Objective Tests

The Objective Tests are a two-hour assessment comprising compulsory questions, each with one or more parts. There will be no choice and all questions should be attempted. The number of questions in each assessment are as follows:

**BA1** Fundamentals of Business Economics – 60 questions

**BA2** Fundamentals of Management Accounting – 60 questions

**BA3** Fundamentals of Financial Accounting – 60 questions

**BA4** Fundamentals of Ethics, Corporate Governance and Business Law – 85 questions

**Information concerning formulae and tables will be provided via the CIMA website: www.cimaglobal.com.**

# SYLLABUS OUTLINE

## BA3: Fundamentals of Financial Accounting

### Syllabus overview

The main objective of this subject is to obtain a practical understanding of financial accounting and the process behind the preparation of financial statements for single entities.

These statements are prepared within a conceptual and regulatory framework requiring an understanding of the role of legislation and of accounting standards. The need to understand and apply necessary controls for accounting systems, and the nature of errors is also covered. There is an introduction to measuring financial performance with the calculation of basic ratios.

Note: Students are required to be aware of the format and content of published accounts but are not required to prepare them. No detailed knowledge of any specific accounting treatment contained in the International Financial Reporting Standards (IFRSs) – including the International Accounting Standards (IASs) – is necessary, except in terms IAS 2 and the treatment of inventory, IAS 16 and IAS 38 for basic non-current asset transactions.

IAS 1 and IAS 7 formats will form the basis of the financial statements. The terminology used for all entities will be that of International Financial Reporting Standards. This will enable students to use a consistent set of accounting terms throughout their studies.

### Assessment strategy

There will be a two hour computer based assessment, comprising 60 compulsory objective test questions. Short scenarios may be given to which one or more objective test questions relate.

### Syllabus structure

The syllabus comprises the following topics and weightings:

| Content area | | Weighting |
|---|---|---|
| A | Accounting principles, concepts and regulations | 10% |
| B | Recording accounting transactions | 50% |
| C | Preparation of accounts for single entities | 30% |
| D | Analysis of financial statements | 10% |
| | | **100%** |

# LEARNING OUTCOMES AND INDICATIVE SYLLABUS CONTENT

## BA3A: Accounting principles, concepts and regulations (10%)

### Learning outcomes

On completion of their studies, students should be able to:

| Lead | Component | Level | Indicative syllabus content |
|---|---|---|---|
| 1. Explain the principles and concepts of financial accounting. | a. Explain the need for accounting records. | 2 | • Accounting records to be kept and their uses; concept of stewardship. |
| | b. Identify the needs of different user groups. | 2 | • Users of accounts and their information needs. |
| | c. Distinguish between the purposes of financial and management accounts. | 2 | • Functions of financial and management accounts; purpose of accounting statements. |
| | d. Explain capital and revenue, cash and profit, income and expenditure, assets and liabilities. | 2 | • Capital and revenue; cash and profit; income, expenditure, assets and liabilities. |
| | e. Explain the underlying assumptions, policies and accounting estimates. | 2 | • Underlying assumptions, policies, accounting estimates; historical cost convention; qualitative characteristics of the Framework, elements of financial statements. |
| | f. Identify the need for and information to be included in an integrated report. | 2 | |
| | g. Describe the accounting equation. | 2 | • The principles and elements of the Framework for integrated reporting. |
| | h. Explain the need for accounting codes. | 2 | • The accounting equation formula. |
| | | | • Use of coding in record keeping. |
| 2. Explain the impact of the regulatory framework on financial accounting. | a. Explain the influence of legislation and accounting standards on published accounting information. | 2 | • Regulatory influence of company law; role of accounting standards; IASs and IFRSs; formats for published accounts. |

# BA3B: Recording accounting transactions (50%)

## Learning outcomes

On completion of their studies, students should be able to:

| Lead | Component | Level | Indicative syllabus content |
|---|---|---|---|
| 1. Prepare accounting records. | a. Prepare the books of prime entry. | 3 | • Record sales, purchase, income and expense transactions in the sales day book, purchase day book, cash book, returns books, and sales/purchase ledger. |
| | b. Apply the principles of double- entry bookkeeping. | 3 | |
| | c. Prepare nominal ledger accounts. | 3 | |
| | d. Prepare the trial balance. | 3 | • The accounting equation; double-entry bookkeeping rules; journal entries. |
| | e. Explain the nature of accounting errors. | 2 | |
| | f. Prepare accounting entries for the correction of errors. | 3 | • Record all types of business transactions in nominal ledger accounts. |
| | g. Prepare accounting entries for non-current assets. | 3 | • Completing the trial balance from given ledger account balances. |
| | h. Prepare a non-current asset register. | 3 | • Errors including those of principle, omission, and commission. |
| | | | • Journal entries and suspense accounts. |
| | | | • In accordance with IAS 16 – acquisition, depreciation (straight line, reducing balance), revaluation, impairment and disposal of tangibles. |
| | | | • In accordance with IAS 38 – intangibles and amortisation. |
| | | | • Information to be recorded in a non-current asset register. |
| 2. Prepare accounting reconciliations. | a. Prepare bank reconciliation statements. | 3 | • Reconciliation of the cashbook to the bank statement. |
| | b. Prepare petty cash statements under an imprest system. | 3 | • Using the imprest system for petty cash. |
| | c. Prepare sales and purchase ledger control account reconciliations. | 3 | • Reconciliation of sales and purchase ledger control accounts to sales and purchase ledgers. |
| 3. Prepare accounting entries for specific transactions. | a. Calculate sales tax. | 3 | • Calculation of sales tax on all business transactions. |
| | b. Prepare accounting entries for sales tax. | 3 | • Accounting entries for sales tax. |
| | c. Prepare accounting entries for payroll. | 3 | **Note:** No knowledge of any specific tax systems/rules/rates will be required. |
| | d. Prepare accounting entries for the issue of shares. | 3 | • Accounting entries for basic payroll information. |
| | | | **Note:** No knowledge of any specific income tax rules will be required. |
| | | | • Issue at full market price, rights issue and bonus issue. |

# BA3C: Preparation of accounts for single entities (30%)

## Learning outcomes

On completion of their studies, students should be able to:

| Lead | Component | Level | Indicative syllabus content |
|---|---|---|---|
| 1. Prepare accounting adjustments. | a. Prepare accounting entries for accruals and prepayments. | 3 | • Calculations and journals for accruals and prepayments (income and expenses). |
| | b. Prepare accounting entries for irrecoverable debts and allowances for receivables. | 3 | • Prepare journals for irrecoverable debts and allowances for receivables from given information. |
| | c. Prepare accounting entries for inventories. | 3 | • In accordance with IAS 2 – calculation of the figure for closing inventory for inclusion in the financial statements (FIFO, LIFO and average cost) and the journal entry to record it. |
| 2. Prepare manufacturing accounts. | a. Prepare basic manufacturing accounts. | 3 | • Manufacturing accounts produced from given information.<br>**Note:** No calculation of overheads and inventory balances is required. |
| 3. Prepare financial statements for a single entity. | a. Prepare financial statements from a trial balance. | 3 | • In accordance with IAS 1 – Statement of profit or loss and other comprehensive income; statement of financial position; statement of changes in equity. |
| | b. Prepare financial statements from incomplete records. | 3 | • Calculate missing numbers using the accounting equation, profit margins and mark-ups, receivables and payables ledgers, and cash and bank ledgers. |
| | c. Prepare a statement of cash flows. | 3 | • In accordance with IAS 7 – operating, investing and financing sections. |

# BA3D: Analysis of financial statements (10%)

## Learning outcomes

On completion of their studies, students should be able to:

| Lead | Component | Level | Indicative syllabus content |
|---|---|---|---|
| 1. Identify information provided by accounting ratios. | a. Identify the information provided by the calculation of accounting ratios. | 2 | • Information provided by accounting ratios. |
| | b. Identify reasons for the changes in accounting ratios. | 2 | • Reasons for the changes in accounting ratios. |
| 2. Calculate basic accounting ratios. | a. Calculation of profitability ratios. | 3 | • Ratios: return on capital employed; gross, operating and net profit margins; non-current asset turnover. |
| | b. Calculation of liquidity ratios. | 3 | • Trade receivables collection period and trade payables payment period; current and quick ratios; inventory turnover. |
| | c. Calculation of risk ratios. | 3 | • Gearing and interest cover. |

Information concerning formulae and tables will be provided via the CIMA website, www.cimaglobal.com.

# Section 1

# OBJECTIVE TEST QUESTIONS

## ACCOUNTING PRINCIPLES, CONCEPTS AND REGULATIONS

### EXPLAIN THE PRINCIPLES AND CONCEPTS OF FINANCIAL ACCOUNTING

1   **Which THREE of the following are accounting conventions?**

   A   Prudence

   B   Consistency

   C   Depreciation

   D   Accruals

2   **Capital maintenance is important for:**

   A   the sources of finance

   B   the measurement of profit

   C   the relationship of debt to equity

   D   the purchase of non-current assets

3   **If, at the end of the financial year, a an entity makes a charge against the profit for stationery consumed but not yet invoiced, this adjustment is in accordance with the convention of:**

   A   materiality

   B   accruals

   C   consistency

   D   objectivity

4   **Drag the correct wording from the following list to complete the sentence regarding the historical cost convention.**

   The historic cost convention_____.

   •   fails to take account of changing price levels over time

   •   records only past transactions

   •   values all assets at their cost to the business, without any adjustment for depreciation

   •   has been replaced in accounting records by a system of current cost accounting

1

**5**    **Drag and drop the following options to complete the statement below.**

In times of rising prices, the historical cost convention has the effect of _____ profits and _____ the statement of financial position asset values

Drag and drop options: overstating, understating (the options can be used more than once)

**6**    **Sales revenue should be recognised only when goods and services have been supplied.**

The accounting convention that governs the above is the:

A    accruals convention

B    materiality convention

C    realisation convention ✓

D    dual aspect convention

**7**    **The term capital maintenance implies that:**

A    the capital of a business should be kept intact by not paying our dividends

B    a business should invest its profits in the purchase of capital assets

C    non-current assets should be properly maintained

D    profit is earned only if the value of an organisation's net assets or its operating capability has increased during the accounting period

**8**    **The accounting convention that requires non-current assets to be valued at cost less accumulated depreciation, rather than their enforced saleable value, is the**

A    net realisable value convention

B    prudence convention

C    realisation convention

D    going concern convention

**9**    **Which THREE of the following are necessary elements of the stewardship function?**

A    To maximise profits

B    To safeguard assets

C    To ensure adequate controls exist to prevent or detect fraud

D    To prepare the financial accounts

E    To attend meetings with the bank

F    To prepare management accounts

**10**    **Which one of the following provides the most appropriate definition of bookkeeping?**

A    To calculate the amount of dividend to pay to shareholders

B    To record, categorise and summarise financial transactions

C    To provide useful information to users

D    To calculate the taxation due to the government

11    Drag and drop the options below into the table provided to identify whether each of the items below would change the capital of a sole proprietor.

- A payable being paid the amount due by cheque

- Raw materials being purchased on credit

- Non-current assets being purchased on credit

- Wages being paid in cash

| Change | No change |
|---|---|
|  |  |
|  |  |
|  |  |
|  |  |

12    In accordance with the IASB® Conceptual Framework for Financial Reporting what is the main aim of financial reporting?

A    To record every financial transaction individually

B    To maintain ledger accounts for every transaction

C    To prepare a trial balance

D    To provide financial information to users of such information

13    The profit of a business may be calculated by using which one of the following formula?

A    Opening capital – Drawings + Capital introduced – Closing capital

B    Opening capital + Drawings – Capital introduced – Closing capital

C    Closing capital + Drawings – Capital introduced – Opening capital

D    Closing capital – Drawings + Capital introduced – Opening capital

14    Do the comments below relate to management or financial accounting? Drag each comment under the correct heading.

|  | Management accounting | Financial accounting |
|---|---|---|
| Uses historical data |  |  |
| Is a legal requirement |  |  |
| Uses both financial and non-financial information |  |  |
| Is normally prepared annually |  |  |

15    Which THREE of the following are qualitative characteristics of financial statements as per the Conceptual Framework for Financial Reporting?

A    Relevance

B    Profitability

C    Comparability

D    Completeness

16 **Select the correct wording to complete each of the following sentences relating to management accounting and financial accounting.**

A  Recording all transactions in the books of accounts is an aim of financial/ management accounting.

B  Providing management with detailed analyses of costs is an aim of financial/ management accounting.

C  Presenting the financial results of the organisation by means of recognised statements is an aim of financial/management accounting.

D  Calculating profit is an aim of financial/management accounting.

17 **Financial accounts differ from management accounts in that they:**

A  are prepared monthly for internal control purposes

B  contain details of costs incurred in manufacturing

C  are summarised and prepared mainly for external users of accounting information

D  provide information to enable the trial balance to be prepared

18 **Which of the following statements gives the best definition of the objective of accounting?**

A  To provide useful information to users

B  To record, categorise and summarise financial transactions

C  To calculate the taxation due to the government

D  To calculate the amount of dividend to pay to the shareholders

## EXPLAIN THE IMPACT OF THE REGULATORY FRAMEWORK ON FINANCIAL ACCOUNTING

19 **Which organisation issues IFRS® Standards?**

A  The International Auditing and Assurance Standards Board (IAASB®)

B  The Stock Exchange

C  The International Accounting Standards Board (The Board)

D  The Government

20 **State whether each of the following statements are true or false.**

|  | *True* | *False* |
|---|---|---|
| International accounting standards are effective only if adopted by national regulatory bodies. |  |  |
| Accounting standards provide guidance on accounting for all types of transaction. |  |  |

# RECORDING ACCOUNTING TRANSACTIONS

## PREPARE ACCOUNTING RECORDS

21 RST had a cash balance of $1,000 on 1 June. During June it sold goods on credit for $5,000 and made a profit of $1,000; it bought goods on credit for $2,000 and paid wages of $400.

**What was RST's cash balance at 30 June?**

$ _600_

22 **If an entity had an increase in receivables of $750, a decrease in the bank overdraft of $400, a decrease in payables of $3,000 and an increase in inventories of $2,000, what would be the change in working capital?**

increase/decrease of $ _6150_ .

23 **The accounting equation can change as a result of certain transactions. Which one of the following transactions would not affect the accounting equation?**

A Selling goods for more than their cost

B Purchasing a non-current asset on credit

C The owner withdrawing cash

D , Receivables paying their accounts in full, in cash

24 **If the owner of a business withdrew cash for her personal use, what journal entry would record this transaction?**

A Dr Capital        Cr Drawings

B Dr Cash          Cr Drawings

C Dr Drawings       Cr Capital

D . Dr Drawings     Cr Cash

25 **Goods withdrawn by a proprietor for his personal use are entered into the accounting records as:**

A . Dr Drawings      Cr Purchases

B Dr Purchases      Cr Drawings

C Dr Capital        Cr Drawings

D Dr Purchases      Cr Sales

26 **A credit balance of $1,834 brought down on BLT's account in the books of ABC means that**

A ABC owes BLT $1,834

B BLT owes ABC $1,834

C ABC has paid BLT $1,834

D ABC is owed $1,834 by BLT

**27** Which one of the following statements is correct?

A    Assets and liabilities normally have credit balances

B    Liabilities and revenues normally have debit balances

C    Assets and revenues normally have credit balances

D    Assets and expenses normally have debit balances

**28** On 1 January, a business had a customer, JKL, who owed $1,200. During January, JKL purchased further goods for $2,100 and returned goods valued at $750. JKL also paid $960 in cash towards the outstanding balance.

What was the balance of JKL's account on 31 January?

A    $1,590 debit

B    $1,590 credit

C    $810 debit

D    $810 credit

**29** What accounting entries are required for ABC to record the return of office equipment that had been purchased on credit from PQR, but not yet paid for?

| | Debit | Credit |
|---|---|---|
| A | Office equipment | Sales |
| B | Office equipment | PQR |
| C | PQR | Office equipment |
| D | Cash | Office equipment |

**30** Which one of the following statements relating to the balance on a ledger account is not correct?

A    A credit balance exists when the total of credit entries is more than the total of debit entries

B    A debit balance exists when the total of debit entries is less than the total of credit entries

C    A credit balance exists when the total of debit entries is less than the total of credit entries

D    A debit balance exists when the total of debit entries is more than the total of credit entries

**31** Which of the following is the correct double-entry to record the purchase on credit of inventories intended for resale?

| | Debit | Credit |
|---|---|---|
| A | Inventories | Receivable |
| B | Inventories | Payable |
| C | Purchases | Payable |
| D | Payable | Purchases |

**32**    X purchases goods from Y on credit and X subsequently pays by cheque. X then discovers that the goods are faulty and cancels the cheque before it is cashed by Y.

**How should X record the cancellation of the cheque in its accounting records?**

|   | Debit | Credit |
|---|---|---|
| A | Payables | Returns outwards |
| B | Payables | Bank |
| C | Bank | Payables |
| D | Returns outwards | Payables |

**33**    When a transaction is credited to the correct purchase ledger account, but debited incorrectly to the repairs and renewals account instead of to plant and machinery account, the error is known as an error of

A    omission

B    commission

C    principle

D    original entry

**34**    An invoice from a supplier for office equipment has been debited to the stationery account.

**What is the effect on profit and non-current assets?**

|   | Profit |   | Non-current assets |
|---|---|---|---|
| A | Decrease | A | Decrease |
| B | Increase | B | Increase |
| C | No effect | C | No effect |

**35**    DEF bought a machine for $15,000 on 1 January 20X1, which had an expected useful life of four years and an expected residual value of $3,000; the asset was to be depreciated on the straight-line basis. On 31 December 20X3, the machine was sold for $4,800.

**What was the amount included in the 20X3 statement of profit or loss account for profit or loss on disposal?**

$_____

**36**    Which of the following statements best defines depreciation in accordance with IAS 16 *Property, Plant and Equipment*?

A    It is a means of determining the decrease in market value of an asset over time

B    It is a means of allocating the cost of an asset over a number of accounting periods

C    It is a means of setting funds aside for the replacement of the asset

D    It is a means of estimating the current value of the asset

37   A business purchased a machine for $120,000 on 1 January 20X3 and another one on 1 July 20X3 for $144,000. Depreciation is charged at 10% per annum on cost, and calculated on a monthly basis.

**What is the total depreciation charge for the two machines for the year ended 31 December 20X3?**

A   $13,200

B   $19,200

C   $21,600

D   $26,400

38   **Which of the following statements is true in relation to the non-current asset register?**

A   It is an alternative name for the non-current asset ledger account

B   It is a list of the physical non-current assets, rather than their financial costs

C   It is part of the double entry bookkeeping system

D   It is a schedule of the cost, date of purchase, location and other information for each individual non-current asset

39   **Which of the following items should be accounted for as capital expenditure?**

A   the assets are shown in the statement of financial position at their original cost

B   The purchase of a vehicle for resale by a car dealer

C   The cost of redecorating an office

D   Legal fees incurred on the purchase of a building

40   EFG bought machinery for $300,000 on 1 January 20X5, and depreciated it at 10% per annum using the reducing balance method.

**What was the depreciation charge for the year ended 31 December 20X7?**

A   $21,870

B   $24,300

C   $27,000

D   $30,000

41    GHI business bought a machine for $72,000 on 1 January 20X0 and another machine for $96,000 on 1 July 20X0. Depreciation is calculated at the rate of 10% per annum on a straight-line basis, calculated on a monthly basis.

**What is the total depreciation charge for the two machines for the year ended 31 December 20X0?**

A    $6,000

B    $8,400

C    $12,000

D    $16,800

42    **In accordance with IAS 38** *Intangible Assets,* **which of the following statements regarding goodwill is not correct?**

A    Goodwill is classified as an intangible non-current asset

B    Goodwill is the excess of the value of a business as a whole over the fair value of its separable net assets

C    Purchased goodwill may be shown on the statement of financial position and is subject to regular impairment reviews

D    Non-purchased goodwill is a liability

43    WXY Ltd purchases a new printing machine. The cost of the machine was $40,000. The installation costs were $2,500 and the employees received specific training on how to use this particular machine at a cost of $1,000. Before using the machine to print customers' orders, a test was undertaken and the paper and ink cost was $500.

**What should be the cost of the machine in the company's statement of financial position?**

$_____

44    **The reducing-balance method of depreciating non-current asset is more appropriate than the straight-line method when**

A    the expected life of the asset is short

B    the asset is expected to decrease in value by a non-current percentage of cost each year

C    the expected life of the asset cannot be estimated accurately

D    it better reflects the pattern of the consumption of the economic benefits derived from the asset

45    **It is important to produce an opening trial balance prior to preparing the financial statements because**

A    it confirms the accuracy of the ledger accounts

B    it provides all the figures necessary to prepare the financial statements

C    it shows that the ledger accounts contain debit and credit entries of an equal value

D    it enables the accountant to calculate any adjustments required

**46** **An error of original entry would occur if the purchase of goods for resale was**

    A     debited and credited to the correct accounts using the incorrect amount in both cases

    B     credited to the purchases account and debited to the supplier's account

    C     debited to a non-current assets account

    D     entered correctly in the purchases account, but entered in the supplier's account using the wrong amount

**47** **Which of the following statements best explains what a cash discount is?**

    A     It is a discount for payments made in cash

    B     It is a discount for payments made by cheque

    C     It is a discount for payments made before the due date

    D     It is a discount for purchases made in bulk

**48** **How is discount allowed to a credit customer accounted for in the financial statements?**

    A     It is offset against discounts received in the statement of profit or loss

    B     It is a reduction in revenue in the statement of profit or loss

    C     It is an expense in the statement of profit or loss

    D     It is a liability in the statement of financial position

**49** **Where, in the financial statements, is discount received classified?**

    A     It is income in the statement of profit or loss

    B     It is offset against discounts allowed in the statement of profit or loss

    C     It is an asset in the statement of financial position

    D     It is disclosed in the statement of changes in equity

**50** **Which of the following statements best explains a trade discount?**

    A     It is a discount granted by the seller to the purchaser for making purchases made in bulk

    B     It is a discount granted by the seller when the customer pays in cash

    C     It is a discount granted by the seller for early settlement of the amount due

    D     it is a discount granted by the seller to overseas customers only

**51** **What is the double-entry to record trade discount allowed to a customer?**

    A     Dr Revenue          Cr Trade discount

    B     Dr Trade discount    Cr Revenue

    C     Dr Purchases        Cr Trade discount

    D     No double-entry is required

**52** **How is carriage inwards accounted for?**

A    It is an expense in the statement of profit or loss

B    It is a liability in the statement of financial position

C    It is income in the statement of profit or loss

D    It is disclosed in the statement of changes in equity

**53** **The double-entry system of bookkeeping normally results in which of the following balances on the ledger accounts?**

|   | Debit balances: | Credit balances: |
|---|---|---|
| A | Assets and revenues | Liabilities, capital and expenses |
| B | Revenue, capital and liabilities | Assets and expenses |
| C | Assets and expenses | Liabilities, capital and revenue |
| D | Assets, expenses and capital | Liabilities and revenue |

**54** **What are the accounting entries required to record sales on credit of $10,000, on which sales tax is applied at the rate of 20%?**

A    Debit Trade receivables' control account $12,000, Credit Sales revenue $10,000 and Credit Sales tax $2,000

B    Debit Trade receivables' control account $10,000, Credit Sales revenue $8,000 and Credit Sales tax $2,000

C    Debit Sales revenue $10,000, Debit Sales tax $2,000 and Credit Suspense $12,000

D    Debit Sales revenue $8,000, Debit Sales tax $2,000 and Credit Suspense $10,000

**55** After calculating XYZ's profit for 20X9, you discover that:

- the purchase of goods for $3,400 had been included in a non-current asset ledger account, and

- interest received of $400 had been credited to sales.

**State the amount by which gross profit and net profit respectively will change when the errors are corrected.**

|   | Gross profit | Net profit |
|---|---|---|
| Increase/decrease | $............. | $............. |

**56** The cash book of BCD has a memorandum column to record settlement discounts when making early payment to suppliers. The column is totalled every week and posted to the nominal ledger.

**What is the correct double entry in the nominal ledger?**

| A | Dr Cash | Cr Discounts received |
|---|---|---|
| B | Dr Cash | Cr Discounts allowed |
| C | Dr Trade payables | Cr Discounts received |
| D | Dr Discounts allowed | Cr Trade receivables |

**57**   An entity received a settlement discount of $1,500 from a supplier. The amount was debited to the discount received account.

**What was the effect of this transaction upon gross profit?**

A   Gross profit is understated by $1,500

B   Gross profit is understated by $3,000

C   Gross profit is overstated by $3,000

D   Gross profit is unaffected

**58**   **A book of prime entry is one in which:**

A   the rules of double-entry bookkeeping apply

B   ledger accounts are maintained

C   transactions are entered prior to being recorded in the ledger accounts

D   subsidiary accounts are kept

**59**   **A suspense account shows a credit balance of $260. Which of the following is a possible reason for the suspense account?**

A   Omitting a sale of $260 from the sales ledger

B   Recording a purchase of $260 twice in the purchases account

C   Failing to write off an irrecoverable debt of $260

D   Recording an electricity bill paid of $130 by debiting the bank account and crediting the electricity account

**60**   A contra entry for $1,912 has been recorded in the accounting records, with the payables' ledger entry being in the account of Harry and the receivables' ledger entry being in the account of Carry. This contra, which should never have been made, is to be cancelled.

**What will the impact of the required correction be?**

|   | Purchase ledger control account | List of supplier balances |
|---|---|---|
| A | No effect | Increase total by $1,912 |
| B | Credit $1,912 | Increase total by $1,912 |
| C | Debit $1,912 | Decrease total by $1,912 |
| D | No effect | Decrease total by $1,912 |

**61** A total, $19,400, from the payments side of the cash book had been posted to the credit side of the payables' ledger control account.

**What journal entry is required to correct this error?**

| | | Debit | Credit |
|---|---|---|---|
| | A | Payables' ledger control $19,400 | Suspense account $19,400 |
| | B | Suspense account $19,400 | Payables' ledger control $19,400 |
| | C | Payables' ledger control $38,800 | Suspense account $38,800 |
| | D | Suspense account $38,800 | Payables' ledger control $38,800 |

**62** **A payment of $240 from petty cash for stationery had been entered in the books twice. What adjustment is required to correct this?**

| | | Debit | Credit |
|---|---|---|---|
| | A | Stationery account $240 | Suspense account $240 |
| | B | Stationery account $240 | Petty cash $240 |
| | C | Suspense account $240 | Stationery account $240 |
| | D | Petty cash $240 | Stationery account $240 |

**63** **Which of the following errors would cause an entry to be made in a suspense account?**

A Rent charges debited to the local business tax account

B Cash paid to a payable debited to the wrong payable's account

C Cash received from a receivable debited to the wrong receivable's account

D Purchase of goods by the business for the proprietor's private consumption debited to purchases

**64** **The purchase of office equipment for $750 had been charged to the purchases account. What adjustment is required to correct this?**

| | | Debit | Credit |
|---|---|---|---|
| | A | Office equipment account $750 | Suspense account $750 |
| | B | Purchase account $750 | Office equipment account $750 |
| | C | Suspense account $750 | Purchase account $750 |
| | D | Office equipment account $750 | Purchase account $750 |

65    Faulty goods returned by a customer with a sales value of $37 had been correctly treated in his personal account and in the receivables' ledger control account, but had been credited to the sales returns account as $73.

**What adjustment is required to correct this?**

|   | Debit | Credit |
|---|-------|--------|
| A | Sales returns account $36 | Suspense account $36 |
| B | Suspense account $36 | Sales returns account $36 |
| C | Sales returns account $110 | Suspense account $110 |
| D | Suspense account $110 | Sales returns account $110 |

66    **Drag the correct word from the following list to complete each of the three statements relating to the identification of errors. Not all words have to be used and words can be used more than once.**

- omission

- commission

- principle

- original entry

A    An error where the wrong amount has been used for both the debit and credit entries is known as an error of _____.

B    An error of _____ is when the correct and incorrect accounts are of different types, for example entered into a SOPL account instead of a SOFP account.

C    An error where one side of the transaction has been entered in the wrong account (but of a similar type to the account and from the same financial statement) is known as an error of _____.

67    After calculating your profit for the year ended 31 December 20X9, you discover the following errors:

- a purchase of inventory which had cost $15,000 had been included in the non-current asset account.

- an electricity bill for $10,000 had been included as rental income rather than as electricity expense.

**Drag and drop words and values from the available list to complete the following statement. Not all words have to be used and words can be used more than once.**

These two errors had the effect of _____ gross profit by $_____ and _____ net profit by _____.

Available words:    overstating/understating/$10,000/$15,000/$25,000/$35,000

68    Would each of the following errors require use of a suspense account to balance the trial balance?  Tick the appropriate box on the table for each error.

| | Suspense account | No suspense account |
|---|---|---|
| The total of the sales book $25,600 has been posted to the sales account as $26,500. | | |
| The purchase of a motor van costing $15,000 has been debited to the purchases account instead of to the non-current asset account. | | |
| The purchase of stationary on credit has been entered into both the stationary account and to the payables account as $54 instead of $45. | | |
| A charity donation of $50 from petty cash has not been entered into the petty cash book. | | |

69    Drag and drop each of the transaction types listed below to match with the appropriate book of prime entry.

- Credit sales
- Credit purchases
- Return of goods sold on credit
- Return of goods bought on credit
- Bank transactions
- Small cash transactions
- All transactions not recorded elsewhere

| Book of prime entry | Transaction type |
|---|---|
| The journal | |
| Petty cash book | |
| Sales day book | |
| Purchases day book | |
| Cash book | |
| Sales returns day book | |
| Purchases returns day book | |

70    Drag and drop words and values from the available list to complete the following statement regarding a cheque transaction.

When transacting business through a bank account using a cheque the _____ makes out a cheque to the _____.  The bank clearing system passes it to the drawer's bank for approval and payment, with the result that it is taken out of the drawer's bank account. This is known as _____ for payment.  Until the cheque is accepted by the drawer's bank, is it considered to be _____ and the bank has the right to return it as _____ if there is something amiss with it.

Available words:

dishonoured/un-cleared/drawer/payee/presenting a cheque

71    The bookkeeping system involves the use of books of prime entry.

**Drag and drop the following transactions into the columns below to indicate the correct book of prime entry for each transaction.**

- The write-off of irrecoverable debts

- The sale of goods for cash

- The sale of goods to a credit customer

| Sales day book | Cash book | The Journal |
|----------------|-----------|-------------|
|                |           |             |

72    **Drag and drop the following elements into the boxes below to correctly state the accounting equation.**

- Assets

- Equity

- Liabilities

$$\boxed{\phantom{xxxxx}} = \boxed{\phantom{xxxxx}} + \boxed{\phantom{xxxxx}}$$

73    **Complete the table of information below to present the accounting equation at the end of day 5.**

Day 1    DEF commenced business introducing $780 cash.

Day 2    Obtained a loan of $300 cash from a family friend.

Day 2    Purchased inventory for $1000

Day 3    Sold goods for $100 cash, which had cost $80 to purchase.

Day 4    Sold goods for $500 on credit, which had cost $400 to purchase.

Day 5    Bought a motor car for $1000 on credit.

| Assets | Equity | Liabilities |
|--------|--------|-------------|
| $      | $      | $           |

74    **Tick the appropriate boxes in the table below to show in which financial statement each of the elements listed would be included.**

| Element | Statement of profit or loss | Statement of financial position |
|---------|:---------------------------:|:-------------------------------:|
| Assets | ☐ | ☐ |
| Liabilities | ☐ | ☐ |
| Expenses | ☐ | ☐ |
| Income | ☐ | ☐ |
| Equity | ☐ | ☐ |

75    Tick the correct boxes in the table below to show whether each of the following transactions would require a debit or a credit entry.

| | Debit | Credit |
|---|---|---|
| Increases in capital/equity | ☐ | ☐ |
| Increase in assets | ☐ | ☐ |
| Decreases in assets | ☐ | ☐ |
| Increases in income | ☐ | ☐ |
| Increases in expenses | ☐ | ☐ |

76    Use the drop down menu within the options below to show the correct debit and credit entry for each of the three transactions.

| Transaction | Debit | Credit |
|---|---|---|
| Purchase of office equipment on credit for $890 | Office equipment/Cash/ Payables/Loan/Purchases | Office equipment/Cash/Payables/Loan/Purchases |
| Sale of inventory for $100 cash | Cash/Sales/Inventory Receivables | Cash/Sales/Inventory Receivables |
| Return of inventory that has been purchased on credit but not yet paid for. | Purchases/Purchases returns/Inventory/Cash/ Payables | Purchases/Purchases returns/Inventory/Cash/Payables |

77    Use the drop down menu within the options below to show the correct debit and credit entry for the following transaction.

ABC purchased goods from DEF on credit. ABC paid for the goods within the agreed credit period of 30 days but subsequently discovered that the goods were not fit for purpose and cancelled the cheque payment before it was cashed by DEF.

**How should ABC record the cancelled cheque?**

| Debit | Credit |
|---|---|
| Payables/Purchases returns/Bank/Sales returns/Receivables | Payables/Purchases returns/Bank/Sales returns/Receivables |

**78** Use the drop down lists available to show the correct accounting entries arising from the totals in the cash payments book below, assuming that control accounts are part of the double entry accounting system.

| Date | Detail | Bank | Discount | Payables | Electricity | Stationery |
|------|--------|------|----------|----------|-------------|------------|
| | | $ | $ | $ | $ | $ |
| 01.01.X7 | XYZ Ltd | 2,900 | 100 | 2,900 | | |
| 05.01.X7 | Admin office | 1,000 | | | 1,000 | |
| 09.01.X7 | Head office | 500 | | | | 500 |
| 15.01.X7 | LMN Ltd | 3,400 | | 3,400 | | |
| 20.01.X7 | Head office | 5,800 | | | 5,800 | |
| | | ——— | ——— | ——— | ——— | ——— |
| | | 13,600 | 100 | 6,300 | 6,800 | 500 |

| Debit/Credit | Account | Value |
|--------------|---------|-------|
| Debit/Credit | Bank/Discount allowed/ Discount received/Payables/ Electricity/Stationery | $13,600 |
| Debit/Credit | Bank/Discount allowed/ Discount received/Payables/ Electricity/Stationery | $100 |
| Debit/Credit | Bank/Discount allowed/ Discount received/Payables/ Electricity/Stationery | $100 |
| Debit/Credit | Bank/Discount allowed/ Discount received/Payables/ Electricity/Stationery | $6,300 |
| Debit/Credit | Bank/Discount allowed/ Discount received/Payables/ Electricity/Stationery | $6,800 |
| Debit/Credit | Bank/Discount allowed/ Discount received/Payables/ Electricity/Stationery | $500 |

**79** ABC has an account in its nominal ledger for FGH which has a debit balance of $1,089.

**Drag and drop words from the list available to complete the following statement:**

_____ owes _____ $1,089. In the ledger of FGH this would represent _____ balance.

Available words: ABC/FGH/an asset/a liability

**80** ABC has a customer, XYZ, who owed it $700 on 1st of January. During January, XYZ purchased additional goods at a cost of $1,500 and returned some unwanted goods which had cost $320. During January XYZ also made a payment towards settlement if its account of $750.

**Drag and drop words from the list available to complete the following statement:**

At 31st of January ABC's ledger accounts would include a _____ balance for XYZ for $_____. This represents _____ to ABC.

Available words: debit/credit/an asset /a liability/430/1880/1770/1130

**81** **Tick the correct boxes in the table below to show whether the following non-current assets would be recognised as tangible or intangible non-current assets.**

| | Tangible | Intangible |
|---|---|---|
| Land & buildings | ☐ | ☐ |
| Motor Vehicles | ☐ | ☐ |
| Goodwill | ☐ | ☐ |
| Machinery | ☐ | ☐ |
| Licences | ☐ | ☐ |
| Patents | ☐ | ☐ |

**82** **Tick the correct boxes in the table below to show whether each of the following items would be recognised as capital expenditure or revenue expenditure.**

| | Capital expenditure | Revenue expenditure |
|---|---|---|
| Replacing a faulty part with a unit which is identical to the original unit. | ☐ | ☐ |
| Replacing a faulty part with a unit which has slightly increased production capacity. | ☐ | ☐ |
| Legal fees for the purchase of land. | ☐ | ☐ |
| Carriage costs for a replacement part for factory machinery. | ☐ | ☐ |
| Costs to build factory extension. | ☐ | ☐ |
| Repainting of head office building exterior. | ☐ | ☐ |

83    Drag and drop the correct options from the list below into the illustration below of all costs which can be capitalized when purchasing a non-current asset in accordance with IAS 16 *Property, Plant and Equipment.*

- Purchase price

- Delivery costs

- Legal fees

- Training costs

- Repairs and maintenance

- Subsequent expenditure that maintains the productive capacity of the asset.

- Subsequent expenditure that enhances the productive capacity of the asset

- Trailing, testing and installation costs.

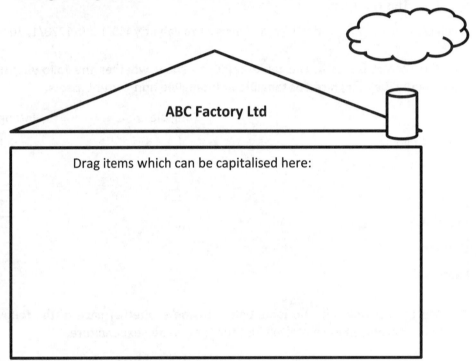

**ABC Factory Ltd**

Drag items which can be capitalised here:

84    Drag and drop the correct options from the list below into the appropriate method of depreciation to fit the asset type.

| Straight-line depreciation | Reducing-balance depreciation |
|---|---|
|  |  |

- Useful for assets which provide equal benefit each year e.g. machinery.

- Useful for assets which provide more benefit in earlier years, e.g. cars, IT equipment.

85    Drag and drop words and values from the available list to complete the following two statements regarding the disposal of a non-current asset.

If the proceeds received on disposal are less than the carrying amount at the date of sale, the difference is a _____ which is treated as _____ when calculating the profit or loss for the year.

If the proceeds received on disposal are more than the carrying about at the date of sale the difference is a _____ which is treated as _____ when calculating the profit or loss for the year.

Available words:    profit on disposal/loss on disposal/an expense/income

86    Using the drop down lists available, show the correct accounting entries at each stage of the process when accounting for the disposal of a non-current asset.

**Step 1 – Remove the asset from the books.**

| Debit | Disposal account/Non-current asset account/ |
| | Cash account/Accumulated depreciation account |
| Credit | Disposal account/Non-current asset account/ |
| | Cash account/Accumulated depreciation account |

**Step 2 – Remove accumulated depreciation from the books.**

| Debit | Disposal account/Non-current asset account/ |
| | Cash account/Accumulated depreciation account |
| Credit | Disposal account/Non-current asset account/ |
| | Cash account/Accumulated depreciation account |

**Step 3 – Record the cash proceeds.**

| Debit | Disposal account/Non-current asset account/ |
| | Cash account/Accumulated depreciation account |
| Credit | Disposal account/Non-current asset account/ |
| | Cash account/Accumulated depreciation account |

87    Using the drop down lists available, show the correct accounting entries at each step of the process when accounting for the disposal of a non-current asset using a part exchange agreement.

**Step 1 – Remove the asset from the books.**

| Debit | Disposal account/Non-current asset account/ Cash account/Accumulated depreciation account |
|---|---|
| Credit | Disposal account/Non-current asset account/ Cash account/Accumulated depreciation account |

**Step 2 – Remove accumulated depreciation from the books.**

| Debit | Disposal account/Non-current asset account/ Cash account/Accumulated depreciation account |
|---|---|
| Credit | Disposal account/Non-current asset account/ Cash account/Accumulated depreciation account |

**Step 3 – Record the part exchange value**

| Debit | Disposal account/Non-current asset account/ Cash account/Accumulated depreciation account |
|---|---|
| Credit | Disposal account/Non-current asset account/ Cash account/Accumulated depreciation account |

**Step 4 – Record the remainder**

| Debit | Disposal account/Non-current asset account/ Cash account/Accumulated depreciation account |
|---|---|
| Credit | Disposal account/Non-current asset account/ Cash account/Accumulated depreciation account |

## PREPARE ACCOUNTING RECONCILIATIONS

88    The petty-cash imprest is restored to $300 at the end of each week. The following amounts were paid out of petty cash during week 23:

| Stationery | $42.30 including sales tax at 20% |
|---|---|
| Travelling costs | $76.50 |
| Office refreshments | $38.70 |
| Sundry payables | $72.00 plus sales tax at 20% |

**What is the amount required to restore the imprest to $300?**

$ ....................

**89**  What effect on a positive cash balance does an adjustment for unpresented paid cheques have on a bank reconciliation?

A    Increase in the cash book balance

B    Decrease in the cash book balance

C    Increase in the balance shown by the bank statement

D    Decrease in the balance shown by the bank statement

**90**  The cash book shows a bank balance of $6,800 overdrawn at 31 July 20X9. It is subsequently discovered that a standing order for $300 has been entered twice, and that a dishonoured cheque for $750 has been debited in the cash book instead of credited.

**What was the correct bank balance at that date?**

$ ....................

**91**  ABC has just completed the following reconciliation of the bank statement to its cash book.

Bank reconciliation statement as at 31 December 20X5

|                                | $       |
|--------------------------------|---------|
| Balance as per bank statement  | 9,564   |
| Add: Unpresented cheques       | 772     |
|                                | 10,336  |
| Less: Uncleared lodgements     | (218)   |
| Balance as per cash book       | 10,118  |

**What figure for cash should be included in the trial balance at 31 December 20X5?**

A    $9,564 Dr

B    $9,564 Cr

C    $10,118 Dr

D    $10,118 Cr

**92**  **A supplier sends you a statement showing a balance outstanding of $6,850. Your own records show a balance outstanding of $7,500. The reason for this difference could be that:**

A    the supplier sent an invoice for $650 that you have not yet received

B    the supplier has allowed you $650 cash discount that you have not recorded in your accounting records

C    you have paid the supplier $650 that he has not yet accounted for

D    you have returned goods worth $650 that the supplier has not yet accounted for

**93** Which of the following items would NOT lead to a difference between the trade receivables' ledger control account and the total of trade receivables' ledger balances?

A An error when totalling the sales day book

B An entry made in the wrong individual receivables ledger account

C An error when totalling the receipts column in the cash book

D Overstatement of an entry in an individual receivables ledger account

**94** Your cash book shows a credit balance of $2,480 at 30 April 20X9. Upon comparison with the bank statement, you determine that there are unpresented cheques totalling $450, and a receipt of $140 that has not yet been passed through the bank account. The bank statement shows bank charges of $75 that have not been entered.

**What was the balance on the bank statement?**

$ _____

**95** An entity's cash book at 31 December 20X4 shows a debit balance of $2,125. When the bank statement is reviewed, it is identified that cheques drawn by the entity totalling $274 had not been presented. In addition, the statement recorded bank charges of $58 which had not been entered in the cash book.

**What was the balance on the bank statement as at 31 December 20X4?**

A $1,909 overdrawn balance

B $1,909 favourable balance

C $2,341 favourable balance

D $2,457 favourable balance

**96** Tick the correct boxes in the table below to show the classification of the following differences between the bank statement and the cash book when performing a bank reconciliation.

| | Unrecorded items | Timing difference | Error |
|---|---|---|---|
| Automated bank charges | ☐ | ☐ | ☐ |
| Unpresented cheques | ☐ | ☐ | ☐ |
| Interest received | ☐ | ☐ | ☐ |
| Dishonoured cheques | ☐ | ☐ | ☐ |
| Direct debits | ☐ | ☐ | ☐ |
| Uncleared lodgements | ☐ | ☐ | ☐ |
| Double charged account fee | ☐ | ☐ | ☐ |

97  Using the drop down lists available show the correct accounting entries required when an entity transfers the daybook totals into the nominal ledger.

Transfer of the sales day book to the nominal ledger

| Debit | SLCA/Sales/Purchases/PLCA/Cash/Bank/Sales ledger account |
|---|---|
| Credit | SLCA/Sales/Purchases/PLCA/Cash/Bank/Sales ledger account |

Transfer of the purchases day book to the nominal leger

| Debit | SLCA/Sales/Purchases/PLCA/Cash/Bank/ Purchase ledger account |
|---|---|
| Credit | SLCA/Sales/Purchases/PLCA/Cash/Bank/ Purchase ledger account |

98  Using the drop down lists available show the correct accounting entries arising from a contra entry

| Debit | SLCA/Sales/Purchases/PLCA/Cash/Bank |
|---|---|
| Credit | SLCA/Sales/Purchases/PLCA/Cash/Bank |

# PREPARE ACCOUNTING ENTRIES FOR SPECIFIC TRANSACTIONS

99  Calculate the sales tax on $100 at a rate of 20%

A   $20.00

B   $16.67

C   $120.00

D   Nil

100  How much is the sales tax amount, if the gross amount invoiced was $6,600, at a sales tax rate of 20%?

A   $7,920

B   $1,100

C   $1,320

D   $5,500

101  X purchased goods costing $500 from Z which had a list price of $500 and which were subject to a trade discount of 20%. Z applies sales tax at the rate of 20% on all sales,

What was the net cost of the goods purchased?

A   $480.00

B   $400.00

C   $600.00

D   $333.33

**102** X purchased goods costing $500 from Z which had a list price of $5,000 and which were subject to a trade discount of 20%. Z applies sales tax at the rate of 20% on all sales.

**How much sales tax was applied by Z on this transaction?**

A $1,000

B $800

C $833.33

D $666.66

**103** TYU purchased goods costing $500 from ZXY which had a list price of $500, and on which were subject to a trade discount of 20%. ZXY applies sales tax at the rate of 20% on all sales.

**What accounting entries should TYU make to record this transaction if it is registered to account for sales tax?**

|   |    |           | $   | $   |
|---|----|-----------|-----|-----|
| A | Dr | Purchases | 400 |     |
|   | Dr | Sales tax | 80  |     |
|   | Cr | Payable   |     | 480 |
| B | Dr | Payable   | 480 |     |
|   | Cr | Sales tax |     | 80  |
|   | Cr | Purchases |     | 400 |
| C | Dr | Purchases | 600 |     |
|   | Dr | Sales tax | 100 |     |
|   | Cr | Payable   |     | 700 |
| D | Dr | Purchases | 480 |     |
|   | Dr | Sales tax | 100 |     |
|   | Cr | Payable   |     | 580 |

**104** **The sales account is:**

A credited with the total of sales made, including sales tax

B credited with the total of sales made, excluding sales tax

C debited with the total of sales made, including sales tax

D debited with the total of sales made, excluding sales tax

**105** An employee is paid at the rate of $20 per hour. Earnings of more than $300 a week are taxed at 20%. Employees' social security contribution is 8%, and employer's social security contribution is 12%. During week 42, the employee works for 45 hours.

**What amounts should be paid to the employee and included in the statement of profit or loss?**

| Paid to employee | Statement of profit or loss |
|------------------|-----------------------------|
| $ _____      | $ _____                 |

106 The correct ledger entries needed to record the issue of $400,000 $1 shares at a premium of 60c, and paid for by cheque, in full, would be

|  | Debit $ | Credit $ |
|---|---|---|
| Bank |  |  |
| Share premium |  |  |
| Share capital |  |  |

107 **Drag and drop words and values from the available list to complete the following two statements relating to discounts.**

_____ are offered by an entity to its customers to increase the volume of sales made.

_____ are offered to encourage credit customers to pay for items quicker than they have previously agreed to.

Available words:    Trade discounts/Cash discounts

108 Use the drop down lists available to show the correct accounting entries to record the following transaction.

STU sold goods with a list price of $3,000 to WXY on a cash basis and allowed WXY a trade discount of 10%.

**How should the transaction be recorded in the books of STU?**

| Debit | SLCA/Sales/Purchases/PLCA/Cash/Discounts Allowed | $3000/$2700/$3300 |
|---|---|---|
| Credit | SLCA/Sales/Purchases/PLCA/Cash/Discounts Allowed | $3000/$2700/$3300 |

109 **Using the drop down lists available show the correct accounting entries arising from the following transactions:**

To record discounts allowed:

| Debit | Revenue/SLCA/Sales/Purchases/PLCA/Discounts received/Cash |
|---|---|
| Credit | Revenue/SLCA/Sales/Purchases/PLCA/Discounts received/Cash |

To record discounts received:

| Debit | Revenue/SLCA/Sales/Purchases/PLCA/Discounts received/Cash |
|---|---|
| Credit | Revenue/SLCA/Sales/Purchases/PLCA/Discounts received/Cash |

**110** TUV purchased goods on credit at a cost of $5,000 and made sales of $4,900 on credit. TUV offers an early settlement discount of 3% to its customers if they pay within 7 days and TUV has been offered an early settlement discount of 2% on its purchases if it chooses to pay within 14 days.

TUV received payment from the customer within 7 days and also paid its supplier within the 14 days early settlement period.

**Using the drop down lists available show the correct accounting entries for TUV to record the discount allowed and discount received based upon the available information.**

**On the sale transaction:**

| Debit | SLCA/Sales/Purchases/PLCA/Cash/Revenue/Discount received | $150/$100/$147/$98 |
|---|---|---|
| Credit | SLCA/Sales/Purchases/PLCA/Cash/Revenue/Discount received | $150/$100/$147/$98 |

**On the purchase transaction:**

| Debit | SLCA/Sales/Purchases/PLCA/Cash/Revenue/Discount received | $150/$100/$147/$98 |
|---|---|---|
| Credit | SLCA/Sales/Purchases/PLCA/Cash/Revenue/Discount received | $150/$100/$147/$98 |

**111 Using the drop down lists available show the correct accounting entries required at each stage of the process when accounting for payroll costs.**

**Step 1 – Gross wages expense**

| Debit | Gross wages expense/Wages payable/Employer SS expense/ SS and income tax payable/Cash paid |
|---|---|
| Credit | Gross wages expense/Wages payable/Employer SS expense/ SS and income tax payable/Cash paid |

**Step 2 – Accounting for employer SS obligation**

| Debit | Gross wages expense/Wages payable/Employer SS expense/ SS and income tax payable/Cash paid |
|---|---|
| Credit | Gross wages expense/Wages payable/Employer SS expense/ SS and income tax payable/Cash paid |

**Step 3 – Accounting for the employee SS and Income tax obligation deducted from gross pay**

| Debit | Gross wages expense/Wages payable/Employer SS expense/ SS and income tax payable/Cash paid |
|---|---|
| Credit | Gross wages expense/Wages payable/Employer SS expense/ SS and income tax payable/Cash paid |

**Step 4 – Accounting for the net pay to employees**

| Debit | Gross wages expense/Wages payable/Employer SS expense/ SS and income tax payable/Cash paid |
|---|---|
| Credit | Gross wages expense/Wages payable/Employer SS expense/ SS and income tax payable/Cash paid |

**Step 5 – SS and Income tax paid to the tax authority**

| Debit | Gross wages expense/Wages payable/Employer SS expense/ SS and income tax payable/Cash paid |
|---|---|
| Credit | Gross wages expense/Wages payable/Employer SS expense/ SS and income tax payable/Cash paid |

**112 Using the drop down lists available show the correct accounting entries for the following pension contribution.**

OPQ earns $1,000 gross in month 3 of the payroll year. Pension contributions have been agreed to be 7% of monthly salary. The ledger entries to record the pension contribution are as follows:

| Debit | Wages payable/Pension liability/Cash/Employer SS expense/SS and income tax payable | $70/$1,000 |
|---|---|---|
| Credit | Wages payable/Pension liability/Cash/Employer SS expense/SS and income tax payable | $70/$1,000 |

**113** An employee is paid a rate of $6 per hour. Earnings of more than $120 a week are taxed at 15%. Employees' SS contribution is fixed at 5% and employer's SS contribution is 7%. During the week ended, the employee worked for 37.5 hours.

**Calculate the amounts to be charged to the statement of profit or loss and paid to the employee in the following scenario.**

| Statement of profit or loss | Paid to employee |
|---|---|
| $_____ | $_____ |

**114 Drag and drop words from the available list to complete the following three statements relating to types of shares available.**

_____ entitle the holders to the remaining distributable profits at the discretion of the directors, after prior interests and claims have been settled.

_____ entitle the holder to a fixed rate of dividend with an instrument which the entity has agreed to buy back from the shareholder at an agreed future date.

_____ entitle the holder to a fixed rate of dividend which ranks ahead of ordinary shareholders for repayment of capital in the event of liquidation of the entity.

Available words:     Ordinary shares/Redeemable preference shares/

Irredeemable preference shares

115 **Drag and drop words from the available list to complete the following three statements relating to share capital terminology.**

_____ is that part of the authorised share capital that has actually been allotted to shareholders following their application for shares.

_____ is that part of the issued share capital paid by shareholders plus any amount that they have agreed to pay in the future.

_____ is that part of the called-up share capital which has been paid by shareholders at a specific date.

Available words:    Issued share capital/Called-up share capital/Paid up share capital

116 **Use the drop down lists available to show the accounting entries to record the following share issue.**

An entity issued 15,000 new ordinary shares with a nominal value of $1 each, at an issue price, in line with market price, of $4 each. The ledger entries to record this are as follows:

| Debit | Bank/Share Capital/Share Premium | $15,000/$45,000/$60,000 |
| Credit | Bank/Share Capital/Share Premium | $15,000/$45,000/$60,000 |
| Credit | Bank/Share Capital/Share Premium | $15,000/$45,000/$60,000 |

117 **Use the drop down lists available to show the accounting entries to record the following share issue.**

An entity issued 10,000 new ordinary shares with a nominal value of $0.50 each, at an issue price of $2. The market price per share immediately prior to the share issue was $2.50. The ledger entries to record this are as follows:

| Debit | Bank/Share Capital/Share Premium | $5,000/$15,000/$20,000/$25,000 |
| Credit | Bank/Share Capital/Share Premium | $5,000/$15,000/$20,000/$25,000 |
| Credit | Bank/Share Capital/Share Premium | $5,000/$15,000/$20,000/$25,000 |

118 **Use the drop down lists available to show the accounting entries to record the following share issue.**

An entity issued 10,000 ordinary shares with a nominal value of $0.75 to its current shareholders free of any contribution from the shareholders. The market price per share immediately prior to the issue was $2. The ledger entries to record this transaction are as follows

| Debit | Bank/Share Capital/Share Premium | $7,500/$12,500/$20,000 |
| Credit | Bank/Share Capital/Share Premium | $7,500/$12,500/$20,000 |

119 Tick the correct boxes in the table below to show which of the following would be recognised as advantages of either a bonus issue or a rights issue. Note – options can be ticked for more than one type of issue.

| | Rights issue | Bonus issue |
|---|---|---|
| Shares are more marketable and more easily transferable due to their lower market value per share. | ☐ | ☐ |
| There is a better chance of the share issue being fully subscribed due to it having an issue price below market price. | ☐ | ☐ |
| It is cheaper than an issue at market price | ☐ | ☐ |

120 **Drag and drop words from the available list to complete the following statement relating to reserves.**

There are two types of reserves, capital reserves and revenue reserves. The difference between these is that capital reserves _____ be distributed as dividends. An example of a capital reserve would the _____ account.

Available words:      may/may not/share capital/retained earnings/share premium

# PREPARATION OF ACCOUNTS FOR SINGLE ENTITIES

## PREPARE ACCOUNTING ADJUSTMENTS

121 BCD paid rent on 1 October 20X2 for the year ended 30 September 20X3 of $600, and paid rent of $800 on 1 October 20X3 for the year ended 30 September 20X4.

**What was the rent payable expense for the year ended 31 December 20X3?**

$..............

122 **NOP commenced business on 1 May 20X0 and is charged rent at the rate of $18,000 per annum.**

During the period to 31 December 20X0 NOP made payments totalling $13,800 for rent.

What should his rent expense be in the statement of profit or loss for the accounting period to 31 December 20X0?

$.............

123 **A decrease in the allowance for receivables would result in**

A    an increase in liabilities

B    a decrease in working capital

C    a decrease in net profit

D    an increase in net profit

**124** CDE measures inventory using the first in, first out (FIFO) basis. Opening inventory comprised 10 units at a cost of $4 per unit. During the accounting period, 30 units were purchased at a cost of $6, followed by issues of 12 units and a further 8 units.

**What was the value of inventory at the end of the accounting period in accordance with IAS 2 *Inventories*?**

$..............

**125** **As referenced in IAS 2 *Inventories*, in times of rising prices, the FIFO method of inventories valuation, when compared with the average cost method of inventories valuation, will usually produce**

A        a higher profit and lower closing inventories value

B        a higher profit and a higher closing inventories value

C        a lower profit and a lower closing inventories value

D        a lower profit and a higher closing inventories value

**126** Inventory movements for product X during the last quarter were as follows:

| | | |
|---|---|---|
| Opening inventories | | 6 items at $30.00 each |
| January | Purchases | 10 items at $39.60 each |
| February | Sales | 10 items at $60 each |
| March | Purchases | 20 items at $49 each |
| | Sales | 5 items at $60 each |

**If inventory is valued using the continuous weighted average cost method, in accordance with IAS 2 *Inventories*, what was the gross profit for the three months ended 31 March?**

$....................

**127** An entity uses the LIFO cost formula. Information regarding inventories movements during a particular month is as follows:

| | | |
|---|---|---|
| 1 | Opening balance | 300 units valued at $3,000 |
| 10 | Purchases | 700 units for $8,400 |
| 14 | Sales | 400 units for $8,000 |
| 21 | Purchases | 600 units for $9,000 |
| 23 | Sales | 800 units for $17,600 |

**What was the cost of closing inventories at the end of the month as per IAS 2 *Inventories*?**

$ ...............

**128** STU sells three products – Small, Medium and Large. The following information was available at the year-end:

|  | Small | Medium | Large |
|---|---|---|---|
|  | $ per unit | $ per unit | $ per unit |
| Original cost | 10 | 15 | 20 |
| Estimated selling price | 14 | 18 | 19 |
| Selling and distribution costs | 1 | 4 | 3 |
|  | Units | Units | Units |
| Units in inventories | 300 | 400 | 600 |

**In accordance with IAS 2 the value of inventories at the year-end should be:**

$ ...............

**129** ABC business had receivables of $1,950 at 1 January 20X3 and $1,200 at 31 December 20X3. $96,750 was received from customers on credit during the year.

**Assuming that there were no irrecoverable debts and no discounts allowed, what were credit sales for the year?**

A    $96,000

B    $96,750

C    $97,200

D    $97,950

**130** LMN had receivables of $300 at 1 January 20X4 and $270 at 31 December 20X4. Credit sales amounted to $2,370 and cash received from receivables was $2,310; an irrecoverable debt of $30 was written off.

**How much discount was allowed to customers during the year?**

A    $60

B    $120

C    $210

D    $270

**131** After the draft financial statements of CDE have been prepared, some inventories are found in an old shed which was not included in the physical inventory count. It appears that they originally cost $1,000, but it was thought that they could be sold for only $100.

**What was the effect on CDE's gross profit?**

A    Increase $100

B    Decrease $900

C    Increase $1,000

D    Decrease $1,000

132 JKL received rent from occupiers of premises during 20X5 of $25,000. Of this, $1,600 related to the year ended 31 December 20X4 and $800 related to the year ended 31 December 20X6. At 31 December 20X5, there was rent due but not yet received on $500.

**What was the rent receivable by JKL for the year ended 31 December 20X5?**

$ ..............

133 An entity received and paid the following rent invoices during the year ended 31 December 20X7:

| 28 Feb | $1,380 |
|--------|--------|
| 31 May | $1,320 |
| 30 Aug | $1,170 |
| 30 Nov | $1,260 |

Additional information:

A rent invoice was received on 28 February 20X8 for $1,350, relating to the period 1 December 20X7 – 28 February 20X8.

**Using the drop down lists available show the correct accounting entries for the year-end journal entry.**

| Debit | Rent expense/Accruals/Prepayments /Bank | $1,350/$450/$900/$390 |
|-------|------------------------------------------|------------------------|
| Credit | Rent expense/Accruals/Prepayments /Bank | $1,350/$450/$900/$390 |

134 An entity received and paid the following rent invoices during the year ended 31 December 20X7:

| 1 Mar | $3,600 |
|-------|--------|
| 1 Jun | $3,600 |
| 1 Sept | $3,600 |
| 1 Dec | $4,500 (to cover period 1st Dec 20X7– 28th Feb 20X8) |

The annual rental was increased to $18,000 per annum with effect from 1 December 20X7.

**Using the drop down lists available show the correct accounting entries for the following year end journal entry.**

| Debit | Rent expense/Accruals/Prepayments /Bank | $4,500/$3,600/$1,500/$3,000/$2,400 |
|-------|------------------------------------------|-------------------------------------|
| Credit | Rent expense/Accruals/Prepayments /Bank | $4,500/$3,600/$1,500/$3,000/$2,400 |

135 An entity rented out a property to a tenant charging $1,500 per month for use of the property. During the year ended 31 December 20X4 the entity received $25,000 cash from the tenant.

**Using the drop down lists available show the correct accounting entries for the following year end journal entry.**

| Debit | Rent expense/Rental income/ Accrued income/Prepaid income/ Bank | $1,500/$2,083/$7,000/$18,000/ $25,000 |
|---|---|---|
| Credit | Rent expense/Rental income/ Accrued income/Prepaid income/ Bank | $1,500/$2,083/$7,000/$18,000/ $25,000 |

136 **Drag and drop words from the available list to complete the following three statements regarding accounting concepts.**

The _____ concept reflects the idea that revenue earning during the accounting period is matched in the statement of profit or loss with the expenses incurred in earning that revenue.

The _____ concept states that we recognise revenue only when it's been earned, not necessarily when cash is received from the customer.

The _____ concept states that revenue and assets should not be recognised unless they can be measured reliably and it is probable that economic benefits will be received.

Available words: accruals/realisation/prudence/going concern

137 **Drag and drop words from the available list to complete the following two statements regarding irrecoverable debts and allowance for receivable.**

_____ would be recognised when information comes to light to suggest that a customer is unwilling or unable to pay their debt in full, or even at all

_____ would be recognised when there is some doubt as to whether some of the entity's receivables may fail to pay their debts in full.

Available words: An irrecoverable debt/An allowance for receivables

**138** Using the drop down lists available show the correct accounting entries resulting from each step of the procedure when reversing a debt which had previously been written off.

Step 1 – Reinstate the debt

| Debit | Receivables/Payables/Bank/Irrecoverable debts/Allowance for receivable |
|---|---|
| Credit | Receivables/Payables/Bank/Irrecoverable debts/ Allowance for receivables |

Step 2 – Recognise the payment

| Debit | Receivables/Payables/Bank/Irrecoverable debts/ Allowance for receivables |
|---|---|
| Credit | Receivables/Payables/Bank/Irrecoverable debts/Allowance for receivables |

**139** Input values and use the drop downs provided show the correct accounting entries arising at the end of December 20X3 given the following information.

The allowance for receivables for each year end was as follows:

| 31 December 20X1 | $5,500 |
|---|---|
| 31 December 20X2 | $8,250 |
| 31 December 20X3 | $10,000 |

| Debit | Cash/Receivables/Allowance for receivables/ Irrecoverable debt expense | $ |
|---|---|---|
| Credit | Cash/Receivables/Allowance for receivables/ Irrecoverable debt expense | $ |

**140** Drag and drop words from the available list to complete the following statement relating to accounting concepts.

Accounting for irrecoverable debts and allowances for receivables represents an application of the _____ concept.  Trade receivables, as an asset in the statement of financial position should not be overstated.

Available words:   going concern/materiality/prudence/accruals

**141** Drag and drop words from the available list to complete the following statements relating to accounting for inventory.

The carry forward of unused inventory is an application of the _____ concept.  This is an extension of the accruals concept.

Available words:   going concern/materiality/prudence/matching

142 Using the drop down lists available show the correct accounting entries required to recognise opening and closing inventory correctly in the financial statements.

Opening inventory brought forward from the previous year:

| Debit | Cost of sales/Inventory asset /Bank/Sales/Purchases |
|-------|------------------------------------------------------|
| Credit | Cost of sales/Inventory asset /Bank/Sales/Purchases |

Closing inventory unused at the end of the accounting period:

| Debit | Cost of sales/Inventory asset /Bank/Sales/Purchases |
|-------|------------------------------------------------------|
| Credit | Cost of sales/Inventory asset /Bank/Sales/Purchases |

143 Which of the following costs should be excluded from the cost of inventory? Select all that apply.

A    Purchase price

B    Delivery costs

C    Production overheads

D    Non-production overheads

E    Storage costs

F    Selling costs

144 Using the drop down lists available in the table below match the following inventory valuation methods to their key points as per IAS 2 *Inventories*.

| Unit cost/ FIFO/LIFO/AVCO | The cost of the closing inventory is the cost of the most recent purchases of inventory. |
|---------------------------|------------------------------------------------------------------------------------------|
| Unit cost/ FIFO/LIFO/AVCO | Used when items of inventory are individually distinguishable and of high value. |
| Unit cost/ FIFO/LIFO/AVCO | The cost of closing inventory is the cost of the oldest remaining items purchased. |
| Unit cost/ FIFO/LIFO/AVCO | This method is used when the average cost can be calculated on a periodic and continuous basis. |

**145** Drag and drop words from the available list to complete the following two statements relating to the weighted average cost inventory valuation method.

_____ weighted average cost is when an average cost per unit is calculated based upon the cost of the opening inventory plus the cost of all purchases made during the accounting period.

_____ weighted average cost is when an updated average cost per unit is calculated following each purchase of goods. The cost of any subsequent sales are then accounted for at that weighted average cost per unit.

Available words:  Periodic/Continuous

---

**The following information is provided for use for questions 146 – 148.**

ABC has closing inventory of 100 units at a cost of $4 per unit as of the 31 December 20X4.  During the first week of January 20X5 they entered into the following transactions:

| Date | Transaction | Units | $ per unit | Total $ |
|---|---|---|---|---|
| 3rd January | Purchased | 120 units | $4.50 per unit | $540 |
| 4th January | Purchased | 200 units | $5.00 per unit | $1,000 |
| 6th January | Sold | 280 units | $7.00  per unit | $1,960 |
| 7th January | Purchased | 100 units | $5.50 per unit | $550 |

---

**146** Calculate the value, as per IAS 2 *Inventories*, of the closing inventory at the end of the first week using the FIFO method of inventory valuation? (round to the nearest full $)

$ ...............

**147** Calculate the value, as per IAS 2 *Inventories*, of the closing inventory at the end of the first week using the periodic weighted average cost method of inventory valuation? (round to the nearest full $)

$ ...............

**148** Calculate the value, as per IAS 2 *Inventories*, of the closing inventory at the end of the first week using the continuous weighted average cost method of inventory valuation? (round to the nearest full $)

$ ...............

**149** In accordance with IAS 2 in times of rising prices, which of the following will give a higher profit in comparison with the other methods?

A FIFO

B Periodic average cost

C Continuous average cost

D All are equal

**The following information is provided for use for questions 150 – 151.**

DEF uses the FIFO method to determine the value of its inventory. At the 1 January it has 20 units of inventory which had cost $15 per unit. During the month of Jan the following transactions took place.

| Date | Transaction | Units | $ per unit | Total $ |
|------|-------------|-------|------------|---------|
| 5th January | Purchased | 50 units | $17.50 | $875 |
| 14th January | Purchased | 80 units | $18 per unit | $1,440 |
| 16th January | Sold | 100 units | $25 per unit | $2,500 |
| 27th January | Purchased | 50 units | $18.50 per unit | $925 |

150 **What was the value of closing inventory at 31 January as per IAS 2 *Inventories*?**

$ ...............

151 **What was the cost of goods sold for January?**

$ ...............

## PREPARE MANUFACTURING ACCOUNTS

152 The following information relates to MNO for the year ended 31 March 20X4:

|  | $ |
|--|---|
| Inventories at beginning of year | |
| Raw materials | 20,000 |
| Work-in-progress | 4,000 |
| Finished goods | 68,000 |
| Inventories at end of year | |
| Raw materials | 22,000 |
| Work-in-progress | 8,000 |
| Finished goods | 60,000 |
| Purchase of raw materials | 100,000 |
| Direct wages | 80,000 |
| Royalties on goods sold | 6,000 |
| Production overheads | 120,000 |
| Distribution costs | 110,000 |
| Administration expenses | 140,000 |
| Sales | 600,000 |

**What was MNO's cost of goods manufactured for the year ended 31 March 20X4?**

$ ...............

**153   If work-in-progress decreases during the period, then:**

  A    prime cost will decrease

  B    prime cost will increase

  C    the factory cost of goods completed will decrease

  D    the factory cost of goods completed will increase

**154   The cost of royalties paid on goods manufactured is included in:**

  A    factory overheads

  B    selling and distribution expenses

  C    prime cost

  D    trading account

**155   The prime cost of goods manufactured is the total of:**

  A    all factory costs before adjusting for work-in-progress

  B    all factory costs of goods completed

  C    all materials and labour

  D    direct factory costs

**156   Which one of the following costs would not be shown as a factory overhead in a manufacturing account?**

  A    The cost of insurance on a factory

  B    The cost of an extension to a factory

  C    The cost of depreciation on a factory

  D    The cost of rent on a factory

## PREPARE FINANCIAL STATEMENTS FOR A SINGLE ENTITY

**157   Which one of the following is not part of the statement of profit or loss?**

  A    Sales

  B    Gross profit

  C    Receivables

  D    Rent receivable

**158   Which of the following items in the statement of financial position would change immediately following a bonus issue of shares?**

  A    Equity share capital and cash

  B    Equity share capital and share premium

  C    Share premium and cash

  D    Share premium and retained earnings

**159** Which one of the following items is not part of the statement of changes in equity?

A Issued share capital at the start of the accounting period

B Retained profit for the accounting period

C Non-current assets

D Revaluation surplus at the end of the accounting period

**160** Which one of the following does not form part of cost of goods sold?

A Closing inventories

B Sales

C Opening inventories

D Purchases

**161** An entity had opening inventories of $400 and closing inventories of $2,000. During the year, it made purchases of $3,000 and made sales of $5,000.

What was the gross profit or loss for the accounting period?

A $3,600 Profit

B $400 Loss

C $10,400 Profit

D $4,400 Loss

**162** An entity had a gross profit for the year of $4,300, and also had the following items included in its trial balance at the end of the year:

• Rent paid $1,000

• Interest paid $300

• Rent received $200

What was the entity's net profit for the year?

A $3,000 profit

B $3,200 profit

C $5,600 profit

D $5,800 profit

**163** When comparing the most recent statement of financial position with that of the previous year, it was noted that inventories had increased by $500, payables had increased by $2,400 and the bank balance had decreased by $800. Receivables were unchanged.

What was the change in working capital?

A a decrease in working capital of $2,100

B an increase in working capital of $2,700

C a decrease in working capital of $2,700

D an increase in working capital of $2,100

**164**  **Gross profit for the year ended 31 December 20X1 can be calculated from:**

A     purchases for 20X1 plus inventories at 31 December 20X1 less inventories at 1 January 20X1

B     purchases for 20X1 less inventories at 31 December 20X1 plus inventories at 1 January 20X1

C     cost of goods sold during 20X1 plus sales during 20X1

D     net profit for 20X1 plus expenses for 20X1

**165**  **What is meant by the term 'working capital'?**

A     Total assets less total liabilities

B     Current assets less current liabilities

C     Capital plus profit less drawings

D     Capital plus profit less drawings plus non-current liabilities

**166**  BCD made sales of $24,000 during the month of January 20X1, incurred expenses of $12,000, and net profit was 10% of sales.

**What was the cost of sales for January 20X1?**

A     $9,600

B     $12,000

C     $14,400

D     $21,600

**167**  **Revenue reserves are defined as:**

A     accumulated and undistributed profits of a company

B     amounts that cannot be distributed as dividends

C     amounts set aside out of profits to replace revenue items

D     amounts set aside out of profits for a specific purpose

**168**  **Which one of the following would you expect to find in the statement of changes in equity of a limited company, for the current year?**

A     Directors' remuneration

B     Ordinary dividend proposed during the current year, but paid in the following year

C     Loan interest payable

D     Ordinary dividend proposed during the previous year, but paid in the current year

169 In a statement of profit or loss and other comprehensive income, the difference between 'profit for the year' and 'total comprehensive income for the year' is:

A    Interest paid

B    Income tax paid

C    Revaluation surplus for the year

D    Dividends paid in the year

170 Which one of the following items would you not expect to find in a statement of changes in equity?

A    Dividends received

B    Transfers between reserves

C    Gains on revaluation of property

D    Issue of shares

171 Revenue reserves would decrease if a company did which one of the following?

A    Repaid a loan

B    Transferred an amount into a 'General reserve'

C    Issued shares at a premium

D    Paid an equity dividend

172 LMN includes the following items as 'reserves' in its financial statements. Which one of them is wrongly classified?

A    Retained earnings

B    Allowance for receivables

C    Revaluation surplus

D    Share premium account

173 With reference to the statement of cash flows, which of the following statements is correct?

A    Dividends declared are an outflow of cash under the heading 'financing activities'

B    Dividends proposed are an outflow of cash under the heading 'financing activities'

C    Dividends paid are an outflow of cash under the heading 'financing activities'

D    Dividends paid are an outflow of cash under the heading 'investing activities'

174 Which one of the following is not a revenue reserve?

A    Retained earnings

B    General reserve

C    A reserve to replace non-current assets

D    Share premium

**175** A statement of cash flows can best be described as:

    A    a statement showing the effects of profit on cash resources

    B    a statement of cash inflows and outflows from operating activities

    C    a statement showing the movement in working capital

    D    a statement showing the inflows and outflows of cash

**176** Revenue reserves would increase if an entity:

    A    issued shares at a premium

    B    made a transfer from retained profit earnings to general reserves

    C    Increased retained earnings

    D    increased its bank balances

**177** Based upon the following information, what was the cost of purchases for the accounting period?

| | $ |
|---|---|
| Opening payables | 71,300 |
| Cash paid to suppliers | 271,150 |
| Discounts received | 6,600 |
| Goods returned | 13,750 |
| Closing payables | 68,900 |

    $ ...............

**178** Based upon the following information, what were the credit sales for 20X3?

| | $ |
|---|---|
| Receivables at 1 January 2003 | 30,000 |
| Receivables at 31 December 2003 | 27,000 |
| Total receipts during 2003 (including cash sales of $15,000) | 255,000 |

    $ ...............

**179** Goods withdrawn by the owner for personal use should be recorded as:

    A    Debit Drawings, and    Credit Purchases

    B    Debit Revenue, and    Credit Drawings

    C    Debit Drawings, and    Credit inventory

    D    Debit Inventory, and    Credit Drawings

**180** Revenue reserves would decrease if an entity:

    A    set aside profits to pay future dividends

    B    transferred amounts into 'general reserves'

    C    issued shares at a premium

    D    paid dividend

# ANALYSIS OF FINANCIAL STATEMENTS

## IDENTIFY INFORMATION PROVIDED BY ACCOUNTING RATIOS

181    **Using the drop down lists provided choose the appropriate words from the available list to complete the following three statements relating to the return on capital employed ratio.**

If an entity revalues its land and buildings the value of the capital employed will increase/decrease.

If an entity has property, plant and equipment which is coming to the end of its expected useful lives, this will result in an increase/decrease to ROCE.

If an entity invests in new property, plant and equipment, this will increase/decrease ROCE in the short term.

182    **Using the table below select from the drop down lists to state whether each of the four scenarios would increase or decrease the gross profit margin.**

| | |
|---|---|
| Sales revenue over the years has remained stable, but costs have increased. | increase/decrease |
| Sales revenue and costs have both decreased but costs by a greater proportion. | increase/decrease |
| There was a change in the sales mix which resulted in a higher proportion of more profitable products being sold in the current year. | increase/decrease |
| The business won new trade discounts with key suppliers. | increase/decrease |

183    **Using the table below select from the drop down lists to state whether each of the four scenarios would increase, decrease or have no impact on average inventory days.**

| | |
|---|---|
| Operating a JIT inventory system. | increase/decrease/no impact |
| Stock-piling inventory in preparation for a new sales drive. | increase/decrease/no impact |
| Increasing sales in the year. | increase/decrease/no impact |
| Negotiating new contracts with suppliers which include increased discounts. | increase/decrease/no impact |

## CALCULATE BASIC ACCOUNTING RATIOS

**184**  **If the selling price of a product was $700, and gross profit mark-up was 40%, what was the cost of the product?**

$ ...............

**185**  **What was the inventory turnover of an entity based upon the following information?**

- Sales were $220,000

- Purchases were $160,000

- Opening inventories was $24,000

- Closing inventory was $20,000.

............... times (to 1 decimal place)

**186**  **The formula for calculating the rate of inventory turnover is:**

A      average inventories at cost divided by cost of goods sold

B      sales divided by average inventories at cost

C      sales divided by average inventories at selling price

D      cost of goods sold divided by average inventories at cost

**187**  **An entity's gearing ratio would increase if:**

A      the decrease in long-term loans is less than the decrease in shareholder's funds

B      the decrease in long-term loans is more than the decrease in shareholder's funds

C      interest rates increased

D      interest rates reduced

**188**  BCD extracted the following information from its statement of financial position:

|  | $000 |
|---|---|
| Inventory | 3,800 |
| Receivables | 2,000 |
| Bank overdraft | 200 |
| Payables | 2,000 |

**Calculate:**

(a)    **the current ratio:_____:1**          State your answer to 1 decimal place.

and

(b)    **the quick (acid test) ratio:_____:1**          State your answer to 1 decimal place.

189   GHI provided the following information for the year ended 31 December 20X7:

| | |
|---|---|
| Inventories at 1 January | $9,075 |
| Inventories at 31 December | $4,500 |
| Purchases | $36,325 |
| Gross profit margin | 30% |

**What was the GHI's gross profit for the year ended 31 December 20X7?**

A     $12,270

B     $13,608

C     $15,567

D     $17,529

**The following information is provided for use for questions 190 – 195.**

The trading account of CDE for the year ended 30 June 20X5 is set out below:

| | $ | $ |
|---|---|---|
| | | 430,000 |
| Sales | | |
| Opening inventories | 50,000 | |
| Purchases | 312,500 | |
| | 362,500 | |
| Closing inventories | (38,000) | |
| Cost of sales | | (324,500) |
| Gross profit | | 105,500 |

The following balances have been extracted from CDE's statement of financial position at 30 June 20X5:

| | $ |
|---|---|
| Trade receivables | 60,000 |
| Prepayments | 4,000 |
| Cash in hand | 6,000 |
| Bank overdraft | 8,000 |
| Trade Payables | 40,000 |
| Accruals | 3,000 |
| Declared dividends | 5,000 |

In questions 190 – 195 assume a year to comprise 365 days and ignore sales tax.

190   **Calculate the inventories days, using average inventories.**

_____days

191   **Calculate receivables days.**

_____days

**192    Calculate payables days.**

_____days

**193    Calculate the current ratio.**

_____:1 (to two decimal places)

**194    Calculate the quick ratio (or acid test ratio).**

_____:1 (to two decimal places)

**195    Calculate the length of the cash cycle in days.**

_____days

---

**The following information is provided for use for questions 196 – 199.**

The following information has been derived from the financial statements of OPQ for the year ended 31 December 20X5.

**At 31 December 20X5**

| | |
|---|---|
| Current ratio | 1.4:1 |
| Quick ratio | 0.9:1 |
| Current assets minus current liabilities | $32,000 |
| Receivables collection period | 6 weeks |

**For the year ended 31 December 20X5**

| | |
|---|---|
| Operating profit for the year as a percentage of ordinary share capital in issue | 40% |
| Annual rate of inventories turnover | 8.775 times |
| Gross profit as a percentage of sales | 25% |

On 31 December 20X5 there were no current assets other than inventories, receivables and bank balances and no liabilities other than current liabilities. Assume a 52-week year.

---

**196    Calculate the value of OPQ's current liabilities on 31 December 20X5.**

$_____

**197    Calculate the value of OPQ's inventories at 31 December 20X5.**

$_____

**198    Calculate OPQ's sales revenue for 20X5.**

$_____

**199    Calculate OPQ's bank balance at 31 December 20X5.**

$_____

**200**   **Which of the following transactions would result in an increase in capital employed?**

   A   Selling inventories at profit

   B   Writing off an irrecoverable debt

   C   Paying a payable in cash

   D   Increasing the bank overdraft to purchase a non-current asset

# Section 2

# ANSWERS TO OBJECTIVE TEST QUESTIONS

## ACCOUNTING PRINCIPES, CONCEPTS AND REGULATIONS

### EXPLAIN THE PRINCIPLES AND CONCEPTS OF FINANCIAL ACCOUNTING

1    **A, B and D.**

Depreciation is not an accounting convention; this is purely an application of IAS 16 *Property, Plant and Equipment*.

2    **B**

Capital maintenance is important for the measurement of profit because the concept states that a profit should not be recognised unless a business has at least maintained the amount of its net assets during an accounting period. Stated differently, this means that profit is essentially the increase in net assets during a period.

3    **B**

The accruals convention implies that the profits must be charged with expenses incurred, irrespective of whether or not an invoice has been received.

4    The historic cost convention fails to take account of changing price levels over time.

Transactions are normally included at their original cost to the business, but that does not preclude reductions in these figures for depreciation and other adjustments. The accounting professions have attempted to introduce systems of current cost accounting in the past, but these have never replaced the historical cost convention. Accounting transactions are always past transactions but not necessarily using the historical cost convention.

5    In times of rising prices, the historical cost convention has the effect of ____**overstating**_____ profits and __**understating**_____ the statement of financial position asset values

**6    C**

The realisation principle, also known as the revenue recognition principle refers to the application of the accruals concept when dealing with the recognition of revenue. This concept states that revenue can only be recognised when the underlying goods or services associated with the revenue have been delivered or rendered, respectively.

**7    D**

The capital maintenance concept states that a profit should not be recognised unless a business has at least maintained the amount of its net assets during an accounting period. Stated differently, this means that profit is essentially the increase in net assets during a period.

**8    D**

The going concern concept is the assumption that an entity will remain trading for the foreseeable future, this means that the entity will not be forced to liquidate or sell off its assets in the near future and so assets should remain at their carrying values and not their enforced saleable value.

**9    B, C and D**

Stewardship is concerned with ensuring that there is a procedure in a place to safeguard assets, provide properly for liabilities, protect against misuse of assets, and report adequately to the shareholders or stakeholders of the organisation.

**10   B**

Bookkeeping is the recording, categorising and summarising of financial transactions.

**11**

| Change | No change |
|---|---|
| wages being paid in cash | a payable being paid the amount due by cheque |
| | raw materials being purchased on credit |
| | non-current assets being purchased on credit |

Transactions that affect only assets and liabilities do not affect capital. Profits increase capital and losses reduce capital.

**12   D**

Items A, B and C are all part of the bookkeeping system. D is the correct answer.

**13   C**

Profit can be calculated as the movement in capital over the course of the year, less any drawings.

**14**

| Management accounting | Financial accounting |
|---|---|
| | Uses historical data |
| | Is a legal requirement |
| Uses both financial and non-financial information | |
| | Is normally prepared annually |

**15    A, C and D**

The qualitative characteristics of the financial statements in line with the IASB Conceptual Framework are relevance, faithful representation, comparability, verifiability, timeliness and understandability.

**16**

Recording all transactions in the books of accounts is an aim of **financial** accounting.

Providing management with detailed analyses of costs is an aim of **management** accounting.

Presenting the financial results of the organisation by means of recognised statements is an aim of **financial** accounting.

Calculating profit is an aim of **financial** accounting.

**17    C**

Financial accounts are summarised as prepared mainly for external users.  A, B and D are all features of management accounts.

**18    A**

The objective of accounting is to provide information which is useful to users.  B, C and D are all uses of the financial statements but they are not the objective.

# EXPLAIN THE IMPACT OF THE REGULATORY FRAMEWORK ON FINANCIAL ACCOUNTING

**19    C**

The International Accounting Standards Board (IASB) issues **IFRS® Standards.**

**20**

| | True | False |
|---|---|---|
| International accounting standards are effective only if adopted by national regulatory bodies. | ✓ | |
| Accounting standards provide guidance on accounting for all types of transaction. | | ✓ |

# RECORDING ACCOUNTING TRANSACTIONS

## PREPARE ACCOUNTING RECORDS

**21**   **$600**

The transactions on credit terms do not affect the cash balance.

**22**   **Increase of $6,150**

The effect on working capital is calculated as

|  | $ |
|---|---|
| Increase in receivables = Increase in working capital | 750 |
| Decrease in bank overdraft = Increase in working capital | 400 |
| Decrease in payables = Increase in working capital | 3,000 |
| Increase in inventories = Increase in working capital | 2,000 |
| | ─────── |
| Overall increase in working capital | 6,150 |
| | ─────── |

**23**   **D**

Receivables paying the accounts in full in cash would not impact on the accounting equation as the transaction both increases and decreases the asset account. The effect is one of reducing receivables while increasing cash, and so the net effect on the accounting equation is nil.

**24**   **D**

The answer is not C because drawings will eventually be transferred to the capital account. The initial entry affects the drawings account.

**25**   **A**

Goods being withdrawn will be removed from purchases as they are not part of the resalable purchases and the equivalent value will be shown as drawings instead. Debit to increase drawings and credit to decrease purchases.

**26**   **A**

A credit balance in the books of A Ltd indicates that it owes money; none of the distracters would result in a credit balance.

**27**   **D**

Assets and expenses normally have debit balances.

Liabilities and revenues normally have credit balances

**28**   **A**

= 1,200 (debit) + 2,100 (debit) − 750 (credit) − 960 (credit) = 1,590 debit

**29** **C**

| *When purchased* | *When returned* |
|---|---|
| Dr  Office equipment | Dr  PQR |
| Cr  PQR | Cr  Office equipment |

**30** **B**

If the total of the debit entries is less than the total of the credit balances then this would reflect a credit balance, not a debit balance.

**31** **C**

The inventories account is never used to record purchases.

**32** **C**

The remove the cheque payment from the books to reflect the cancellation X needs to reverse the original entry.

On payment of the cheque X would have recorded a Dr to payables and a Cr to the bank. To reverse this entry X should Dr Bank and Cr Payables.

**33** **C**

This is a straightforward test of your knowledge of types of errors that can exist. If the wrong account is used, and this results in an incorrect statement of profit, then an error of principle has been made. Debiting the repairs and renewals account results in an extra charge for expenses in the statement of profit or loss, when the item should be included as a non-current asset on the statement of financial position.

**34** **A, C**

Profits:  A  Decrease

Non-current assets:  C  No effect

**35** **Loss of $1,200**

The profit or loss on disposal is the difference between the carrying amount at the time of disposal and the disposal proceeds. An excess of disposal proceeds over carrying amount indicates a profit on disposal, while an excess of carrying amount over disposal proceeds indicates a loss on disposal.

The annual depreciation on the machine is calculated as:

$$\frac{\text{Cost} - \text{residual value}}{\text{Useful economic life}} = \frac{15,000 - 3,000}{4 \text{ years}} = \$3,000 \text{ per year}$$

**Non-current asset disposal account**

| Cost | 15,000 | Accumulated depreciation | 9,000 |
|------|--------|--------------------------|-------|
|      |        | Sale proceeds            | 4,800 |
|      |        | Loss                     | 1,200 |
|      | _____ |                          | _____ |
|      | 15,000 |                          | 15,000 |
|      | _____ |                          | _____ |

**36    B**

Depreciation never provides a fund for the replacement of the asset, nor does it aim to show assets at their fair values.

**37    B**

|  | $ |
|--|---|
| Machine 1: $120,000 × 10% | 12,000 |
| Machine 1: $144,000 × 10% × 6/12 | 7,200 |
|  | _____ |
|  | 19,200 |
|  | _____ |

**38    D**

The non-current asset register is an itemised schedule of non-current assets that will include information for each asset such as cost, date of purchase, location, serial or identification number, depreciation method and rate.

**39    D**

The only item that should be capitalised is the legal costs incurred on the purchase of a building. All of the remaining items are revenue expenses.

**40    B**

|  | $ |
|--|---|
| Cost | 300,000 |
| Depreciation 10% 20X5 | (30,000) |
|  | _____ |
|  | 270,000 |
| Depreciation 10% 20X6 | (27,000) |
|  | _____ |
|  | 243,000 |
| Depreciation 10% 20X7 | (24,300) |
|  | _____ |

**41    C**

Machine 1: Cost 72,000 × 10% = 7,200

Machine 2: Cost 96,000 × 10% = 9,600 × 6/12 = 4,800

Total 7,200 + 4,800 = $12,000

**42    D**

A, B and C are correct in most situations. Non-purchased goodwill would not be recorded.

**43    $43,000**

|  | $ |
|---|---|
| Cost of machine | 40,000 |
| Installation | 2,500 |
| Testing | 500 |
|  | 43,000 |

**44    D**

The reducing balance method should be used to depreciate assets which have a reducing benefit over the course of their lives. This matches the reducing benefit with a reduced expense.

**45    C**

An opening trial balance will prove that the ledgers have equal debit and credit entries; it won't however prove accuracy because there could be errors contained which still allow the trial balance to balance. The opening trial balance does not give all the figures necessary because year-end adjustments still need to be processed.

**46    A**

An error of original entry occurs when an incorrect amount is posted to the correct accounts. This is the case in A only.

**47    C**

A cash discount is a discount for early settlement or prompt payment of an invoice.

**48    B**

Discount allowed is a reduction in revenue in the statement of profit or loss.

**49    A**

Discount received is a form of income and so would be recognised in the statement of profit or loss.

**50    A**

A trade discount is given as a reduction to the published list price of a product, usually to encourage customers to purchase bigger quantities and bulk buying.

**51    D**

No double entry is required – trade discount is already deducted from the initial amount at the pint an invoice is prepared

**52    A**

Carriage inwards is the cost of transporting goods purchased into the business.

**53    C**

Remember to include capital (equity) when considering ledger account balances.

**54    A**

|        | Ledger Account:                                  | $      |
|--------|--------------------------------------------------|--------|
| Debit  | Trade receivables' ledger control account        | 12,000 |
| Credit | Sales                                            | 10,000 |
| Credit | Sales tax                                        | 2,000  |

**55**

|          | Gross profit | Net profit |
|----------|--------------|------------|
| Decrease | $3,800       | $3,400     |

**56    C**

Discounts allowed by BCD's suppliers are discounts received in their records. A discount received is a form of income which reduces the amount payable. This would be recorded as a Dr to reduce payables and Cr to discounts received to recognise the income on the statement of profit or loss.

**57    D**

Discount received is stated in the statement of profit or loss rather than trading account, therefore the net profit will be affected by $3,000, but the gross profit is not affected.

**58    C**

A is incorrect as the journal is one of the books of prime entry in which double-entry rules do apply. B is incorrect as ledger accounts are not maintained in books of prime entry. D is incorrect as subsidiary accounts are ledger accounts that are maintained outside the main ledgers.

**59    B**

A credit balance on the suspense account indicates that the debit total of the trial balance was higher than the credit total. An error that could cause this would involve either too great a value having been debited, too little a value have been credited, or a combination of these where an item has been recorded as a debit when it ought to have been a credit.

A      would result in too little having been debited to the customer's account

B      would result in an additional debit entry, therefore this is the correct answer

C      would not cause any imbalance in the trial balance as both the debit and credit entries will have been omitted

D      would not cause any imbalance in the trial balance as both a debit and a credit entry have been made even though they were the wrong way round

**60    B**

A contra entry is used to reduce receivables and reduce payables.  A contra entry should be recorded both in the nominal ledger and in the memorandum accounts.   If the entry is to be reversed then the effect will be to increase both the PLCA and the SLCA and to increase the list of balances for both customers and suppliers.

To increase the PLCA there would be a credit entry of $1,912 and the supplier list of balances would be increased by $1,912.

**61    C**

This transaction should have been debited to the payables ledger control account.  The incorrect credit entry would have resulted in a debit balance in the suspense account.  To remove the incorrect entry to the payables ledger control account a Dr of $19,400 and then a further Dr of $19,400 to post to correct entry.  Total debit entry to PLCA required is $38,800 and a matching Cr entry to suspense.

**62    D**

One of the entries needs to be removed.  This is achieved with a Debit to petty cash and a Credit to stationary for $240.

**63    C**

A suspense account would be created when transactions are posted to the ledgers with unequal debits and credits.  This would be the case in C as the cash received should be been credited to the receivables account.  A debit to the receivables account will have the result of a debit entry to both cash and to receivables, and a suspense account would have been opened to balance the credit side.

**64    D**

This transaction should have been debited to the office equipment account not to purchases.  The incorrect entry should be removed from purchases with a Cr entry to purchases then posted correctly into the office equipment account with a Dr entry to office equipment.

**65    C**

This transaction should have been debited to sales returns. The incorrect credit entry will have resulted in a suspense account being created. To remove the incorrect entry to sales returns a Dr entry of $73 is required and then to post the correct entry a further Dr of $37 to sales returns. Total Dr entry to sales returns required is $110 and an equal entry Cr to the suspense account.

**66**    An error where the wrong amount has been used for both the debit and credit entries is known as an error of **original entry.**

An error of **principle** is when the correct and incorrect accounts are of different types, for example entered into a SOPL account instead of a SOFP account.

An error where one side of the transaction has been entered in the wrong account (but of a similar type to the account and from the same financial statement) is known as an error of **commission**.

**67**    These two errors had the effect of **overstating** gross profit by **$15,000**

and **overstating** net profit by **$35,000**.

**68**

|  | Suspense account | No suspense account |
|---|---|---|
| The total of the sales book $25,600 has been posted to the sales account as $26,500. | ✓ | |
| The purchase of a motor van costing $15,000 has been debited to the purchases account instead of to the non-current asset account. | | ✓ |
| The purchase of stationary on credit has been entered into both the stationary account and to the payables account as $54 instead of $45. | | ✓ |
| A charity donation of $50 from petty cash has not been entered into the petty cash book. | ✓ | |

**69**

| Book of prime entry | Transaction type |
|---|---|
| The journal | All transactions not recorded elsewhere |
| Petty cash book | Small cash transactions |
| Sales day book | Credit sales |
| Purchases day book | Credit purchases |
| Cash book | Bank transactions |
| Sales returns day book | Return of goods sold on credit |
| Purchases returns day book | Return of goods bought on credit |

**70**   When transacting business through a bank account using a cheque the **drawer** makes out a cheque to the **payee**. The bank clearing system passes it to the drawer's bank for approval and payment, with the result that it is taken out of the drawer's bank account. This is known as **presenting a cheque** for payment. Until the cheque is accepted by the drawers bank, is it considered to be **un-cleared** and the bank has the right to return it as **dishonored** if there is something amiss with it.

**71**

| Sales day book | Cash book | The Journal |
|---|---|---|
| The sale of goods to a credit customer | The sale of goods for cash | The write-off of irrecoverable debts |

**72**

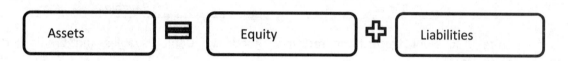

**73**

| Assets | Equity | Liabilities |
|---|---|---|
| $2,200 | $900 | $1,300 |

**74**

| Element | Statement of profit or loss | Statement of financial position |
|---|---|---|
| Assets | ☐ | ✓ |
| Liabilities | ☐ | ✓ |
| Expenses | ✓ | ☐ |
| Income | ✓ | ☐ |
| Equity | ☐ | ✓ |

**75**

| | Debit | Credit |
|---|---|---|
| Increases in capital/equity | ☐ | ✓ |
| Increase in assets | ✓ | ☐ |
| Decreases in assets | ☐ | ✓ |
| Increases in income | ☐ | ✓ |
| Increases in expenses | ✓ | ☐ |

**76**

| Transaction | Debit | Credit |
|---|---|---|
| Purchase of office equipment on credit for $890 | Office equipment | Payables |
| Sale of inventory for $100 cash | Cash | Sales |
| Return of inventory that has been purchased on credit but not yet paid for. | Payables | Purchases returns |

**77**

| Debit | Credit |
|---|---|
| Bank | Payables |

Note: ABC would record the return of goods as: Debit Payables and Credit Returns Outwards.

**78**

| Debit/Credit | Account | Value |
|---|---|---|
| Credit | Bank | $13,600 |
| Debit | Payables | $100 |
| Credit | Discount received | $100 |
| Debit | Payables | $6,300 |
| Debit | Electricity | $6,800 |
| Debit | Stationery | $500 |

**79** **FGH** owes **ABC** $1,089. In the ledger of FGH this would represent **a liability** balance.

**80** At 31 January ABC's ledger accounts would include a debit balance for XYZ for $1,130. This represents an asset to ABC.

**81**

| | Tangible | Intangible |
|---|---|---|
| Land & buildings | ✓ | ☐ |
| Motor Vehicles | ✓ | ☐ |
| Goodwill | ☐ | ✓ |
| Machinery | ✓ | ☐ |
| Licences | ☐ | ✓ |
| Patents | ☐ | ✓ |

**82**

| | Capital expenditure | Revenue expenditure |
|---|:---:|:---:|
| Replacing a faulty part with a unit which is identical to the original unit. | ☐ | ✓ |
| Replacing a faulty part with a unit which has slightly increased production capacity. | ✓ | ☐ |
| Legal fees for the purchase of land. | ✓ | ☐ |
| Carriage costs for a replacement part for factory machinery. | ☐ | ✓ |
| Costs to build factory extension. | ✓ | ☐ |
| Repainting of head office building exterior. | ☐ | ✓ |

**83**

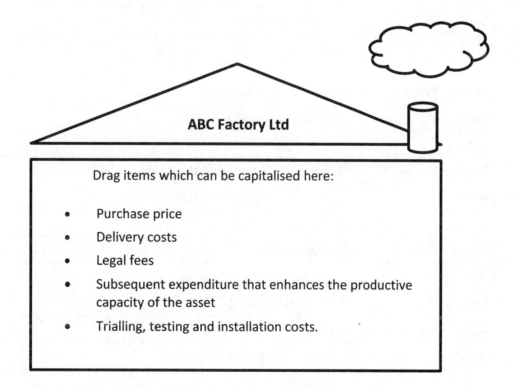

**ABC Factory Ltd**

Drag items which can be capitalised here:

- Purchase price
- Delivery costs
- Legal fees
- Subsequent expenditure that enhances the productive capacity of the asset
- Trialling, testing and installation costs.

**84**

| Straight-line depreciation | Reducing-balance depreciation |
|---|---|
| • Useful for assets which provide equal benefit each year e.g. machinery. | • Useful for assets which provide more benefit in earlier years, e.g. cars, IT equipment. |

**85**    If the proceeds received on disposal are less than the carrying amount at the date of sale, the difference is a **loss on disposal** which is treated as **an expense** when calculating the profit or loss for the year.

If the proceeds received on disposal are more than the carrying about at the date of sale the difference is a **profit on disposal** which is treated as **income** when calculating the profit or loss for the year.

**86**

**Step 1 – Remove the asset from the books.**

| Debit | Disposal account |
|---|---|
| Credit | Non-current asset account |

**Step 2 – Remove accumulated depreciation from the books.**

| Debit | Accumulated depreciation account |
|---|---|
| Credit | Disposal account |

**Step 3 – Record the cash proceeds.**

| Debit | Cash account |
|---|---|
| Credit | Disposal account |

**87**

**Step 1 – Remove the asset from the books.**

| Debit | Disposal account |
|---|---|
| Credit | Non-current asset account |

**Step 2 – Remove accumulated depreciation from the books.**

| Debit | Accumulated depreciation account |
|---|---|
| Credit | Disposal account |

**Step 3 – Record the part exchange value**

| Debit | Non-current asset account |
|---|---|
| Credit | Disposal account |

**Step 4 – Record the remainder**

| Debit | Non-current asset account |
|---|---|
| Credit | Cash account |

## PREPARE ACCOUNTING RECONCILIATIONS

**88** **$243.90**

|  | $ |
|---|---|
| Stationery | 42.30 |
| Travelling cost | 76.50 |
| Refreshments | 38.70 |
| Sundry payables ($72.00 × 1.2) | 86.40 |
|  | 243.90 to restore to 300 |

**89** **D**

Unpresented cheques have been recorded correctly as a reduction in the cash book but since they have not yet been presented by suppliers to the bank, the bank statement is overstated; to reconcile this difference a decrease in the balance shown on the bank statement is required.

**90** **$8,000 OVERDRAWN**

$(6,800) + 300 - (750 \times 2) = (8,000)$

**91** **D**

The nature of the reconciliation indicates that ABC has an overdraft. For example, unpresented cheques have an adverse effect on the bank balance, here they are increasing therefore the bank account is overdrawn.

**92** **B**

If the supplier believes that we owe less than we have recorded on our own ledgers this could be the result of them offering us a discount which we have not entered into our records. This would be recorded as discount received in your accounting records.

A, C and D would result in them having a higher balance owing than we are showing in our records.

**93** **B**

All other items would result an error in either the total of the trade receivables' ledger control account, or an error in the total of the receivables' ledger balances. Item B, will result in errors to two individual receivables' ledger account balances; one will be overstated and the other understated by the same amount.

**94    $2,245 OVERDRAWN**

|  | $ |
|---|---|
| Cash book balance | (2,480) |
| Unpresented cheques | 450 |
| Receipt not yet processed | (140) |
| Bank charges | (75) |
|  | _____ |
| As per statement | (2,245) |
|  | _____ |

**95    C**

2,125 + 274 − 58 = 2,341

**96**

|  | Unrecorded items | Timing difference | Error |
|---|---|---|---|
| Automated bank charges | ✓ | ☐ | ☐ |
| Unpresented cheques | ☐ | ✓ | ☐ |
| Interest received | ✓ | ☐ | ☐ |
| Dishonoured cheques | ✓ | ☐ | ☐ |
| Direct debits | ✓ | ☐ | ☐ |
| Uncleared lodgements | ☐ | ✓ | ☐ |
| Double charged account fee | ☐ | ☐ | ✓ |

**97    Transfer of the sales day book to the nominal ledger**

| Debit | SLCA |
|---|---|
| Credit | Sales |

**Transfer of the purchases day book to the nominal leger**

| Debit | Purchases |
|---|---|
| Credit | PLCA |

**98**

| Debit | PLCA |
|---|---|
| Credit | SLCA |

## PREPARE ACCOUNTING ENTRIES FOR SPECIFIC TRANSACTIONS

**99**  **A**

$100 × 20% = $20

**100**  **B**

$6,600 × 20/120 = $1,100

**101**  **B**

|  | $ |
|---|---|
| List price | 500 |
| Less: Trade discount | (100) |
| Purchases | 400 |

**102**  **B**

|  | $ |
|---|---|
| List price | 5,000.00 |
| Less: Trade discount | (1,000.00) |
| Net purchases | 4,000.00 |
| Sales tax @ 20% | 800.00 |
|  | 4,800.00 |

**103**  **A**

|  |  | $ | $ |
|---|---|---|---|
| Dr | Purchases | 400 |  |
| Dr | Sales tax | 80 |  |
| Cr | Payable |  | 480 |

**104**  **B**

Sales tax is excluded from sales and purchases accounts, so items A and C are incorrect. Sales is a category of revenue, and therefore the sales account is credited.

**105 $708 and $1,008**

|  | Hours |  | $ |
|---|---|---|---|
| Gross pay | $20 | 45 | 900 |
|  | ___ | ___ |  |
| Tax |  | 900 |  |
| Threshold |  | (300) |  |
|  |  | ___ |  |
|  | 20% | 600 | (120) |
|  | ___ | ___ |  |
| Employee SS | 8% | 900 | (72) |
| **Paid to employee** |  |  | **708** |
|  |  |  | ___ |
| Wages IS |  |  | 900 |
| Employer SS | 12% | 900 | 108 |
|  |  |  | ___ |
| **Statement of profit or loss charge** |  |  | **1,008** |
|  |  |  | ___ |

**106**

|  | Debit | Credit |
|---|---|---|
| Bank | 640,000 |  |
| Share premium |  | 240,000 |
| Share capital |  | 400,000 |

**107** **Trade discounts** are offered by an entity to its customers to increase the volume of sales made.

**Cash discounts** are offered to encourage credit customers to pay for items quicker than they have previously agreed to.

**108**

| Debit | Cash | $2,700 |
|---|---|---|
| Credit | Sales | $2,700 |

**109**

To record discounts allowed:

| Debit | Revenue |
|---|---|
| Credit | SLCA |

To record discounts received:

| Debit | PLCA |
|---|---|
| Credit | Discounts received |

**110**

Sale transaction:

| Debit | Revenue ($4,900 × 3%) | $147 |
|---|---|---|
| Credit | SLCA | $147 |

Purchase transaction:

| Debit | PLCA | $100 |
|---|---|---|
| Credit | Discount received ($5,000 × 2%) | $100 |

**111**

**Step 1 – Gross wages expense**

| Debit | Gross wages expense |
|---|---|
| Credit | Wages payable |

**Step 2 – Accounting for employer SS obligation**

| Debit | Employer SS expense |
|---|---|
| Credit | SS and income tax payable |

**Step 3 – Accounting for the employee SS and Income tax obligation deducted from gross pay**

| Debit | Wages payable |
|---|---|
| Credit | SS and income tax payable |

**Step 4 – Accounting for the net pay to employees**

| Debit | Wages payable |
|---|---|
| Credit | Cash paid |

**Step 5 – SS and Income tax paid to the tax authority**

| Debit | SS and income tax payable |
|---|---|
| Credit | Cash paid |

**112**

| Debit | Wages payable | $70 |
|---|---|---|
| Credit | Pension liability | $70 |

**113**

| Statement of profit or loss | Paid to employee |
|---|---|
| $15.75 + $225 = $240.75 | $225 - $11.25 - $15.75 = $198 |

**114**

**Ordinary shares** entitle the holders to the remaining distributable profits at the discretion of the directors, after prior interests and claims have been settled.

**Redeemable preference shares** entitle the holder to a fixed rate of dividend with an instrument which the entity has agreed to buy back from the shareholder at an agreed future date.

**Irredeemable preference shares** entitle the holder to a fixed rate of dividend which ranks ahead of ordinary shareholders for repayment of capital in the event of liquidation of the entity

**115**

**Issued share capital** is that part of the authorised share capital that has actually been allotted to shareholders following their application for shares.

**Called up share capital** is that part of the issued share capital paid by shareholders plus any amount that they have agreed to pay in the future.

**Paid up share capital** is that part of the called-up share capital which has been paid by shareholders at a specific date.

**116**

| Debit | Bank | $60,000 |
|---|---|---|
| Credit | Share Capital | $15,000 |
| Credit | Share Premium | $45,000 |

**117**

| Debit | Bank | $20,000 |
|---|---|---|
| Credit | Share Capital | $5,000 |
| Credit | Share Premium | $15,000 |

**118**

| Debit | Share Premium | $7,500 |
|---|---|---|
| Credit | Share Capital | $7,500 |

**119**

| | Rights issue | Bonus issue |
|---|---|---|
| Shares are more marketable and more easily transferable due to their lower market value per share. | ✓ | ✓ |
| There is a better chance of the share issue being fully subscribed due to it having an issue price below market price. | ✓ | |
| It is cheaper than an issue at market price. | ✓ | ✓ |

**120**

There are two types of reserves, capital reserves and revenue reserves. The difference between these is that capital reserves **may not** be distributed as dividends. An example of a capital reserve would be the **share premium** account.

# PREPARATION OF ACCOUNTS FOR SINGLE ENTITIES

## PREPARE ACCOUNTING ADJUSTMENTS

### 121 $650

The year to 31 December 20X3 includes 3/4 of the rent for the year to 30 September 20X3 and 1/4 of the rent for the year to 30 September 20X4, that is:

$(3/4 \times \$600) + (1/4 \times \$800) = \$650$

### 122 $12,000

$(8/12 \times \$18,000) = \$12,000$

### 123 D

The change in allowance for receivables is taken to the statement of profit or loss – an increase is debited and therefore decreases net profit, whilst a decrease is credited and therefore increases net profit. The resulting balance on the allowance for receivables account is deducted from receivables (current assets), which in turn affects working capital. A decrease in the allowance would increase net profit, and would increase current assets. The latter is not one of the options, therefore D is the answer.

### 124 $120.00

Closing inventory = 10 + 30 – 12 – 8 = 20 units, each valued at a cost of $6.00.

### 125 B

The closing inventories figure reduces the cost of goods sold figure, which in turn increases the gross profit.

Therefore, a higher closing inventories figure means a lower cost of goods sold figure, and hence a higher gross profit. In times of rising prices, the FIFO method of inventories valuation will produce higher closing inventories values, and therefore higher gross profit figure.

## 126 $310

Summarised inventory card

|  | Quantity | Value ($) |  |
|---|---|---|---|
| 6 × $30 | 6 | 180 | |
| 10 × $39.60 | 10 | 396 | |
| | 16 | 576 | ($36 each) |
| 10 × $36 | (10) | (360) | |
| | 6 | 216 | |
| 20 × $49 | 20 | 980 | |
| | 26 | 1,196 | ($46 each) |
| 5 × $46 | (5) | (230) | |
| | 21 | 966 | |

**Note:** Issues are shown in brackets

Trading account

| | $ | $ |
|---|---|---|
| Sales (15 × $60) | | 900 |
| Opening inventories | 180 | |
| Add: Purchases | 1,376 | |
| (396 + 980) | | |
| | 1,556 | |
| Less: Closing inventories | (966) | |
| | | (590) |
| Profit | | 310 |

## 127 $4,200

Closing inventory = 300 + 700 − 400 + 600 − 800 = 400 units. They are valued as follows:

300 units at $10 = $3,000 plus 100 units at $12 = $1,200, giving a total valuation of $4,200.

## 128 $18,200

Lower of cost and net realisable value

| | Units | $ | $ |
|---|---|---|---|
| Small | 300 | 10 | 3,000 |
| Medium | 400 | 14 | 5,600 |
| Large | 600 | 16 | 9,600 |
| | | | 18,200 |

**129 A**

**Receivables control**

| | $ | | $ |
|---|---|---|---|
| Bal b/d | 1,950 | Cash | 96,750 |
| Sales (Balancing figure) | 96,000 | Bal c/d | 1,200 |
| | 97,950 | | 97,950 |

**130 A**

**Receivables control**

| | $ | | $ |
|---|---|---|---|
| Bal b/d | 300 | Cash | 2,310 |
| Sales | 2,370 | Irrecoverable debts written off | 30 |
| | | Discount allowed (bal. fig.) | 60 |
| | | Bal c/d | 270 |
| | 2,670 | | 2,670 |

**131 A**

Omitted from closing inventories, therefore its inclusion will increase profit by the lower of cost and net realisable value, i.e. $100.

**132 $23, 100**

**Rent Receivable**

| | $ | | $ |
|---|---|---|---|
| Bal b/f | 1,600 | Cash received | 25,000 |
| Profit or loss | 23,100 | | |
| Balance c/f | 800 | Balance c/f | 500 |
| | 25,500 | | 25,500 |

**133**

| Debit | Rent expense | $450 |
|---|---|---|
| Credit | Accruals | $450 |

**134**

| Debit | Prepayments | $3,000 |
|---|---|---|
| Credit | Rent | $3,000 |

**135**

| Debit | Rental income | $7,000 |
|-------|---------------|--------|
| Credit | Prepaid income | $7,000 |

**136**

The **accruals** concept reflects the idea that revenue earning during the accounting period is matched in the statement of profit or loss with the expenses incurred in earning that revenue.

The **realisation** concept states that we recognise revenue only when it's been earned, not necessarily when cash is received from the customer.

The **prudence** concept states that revenue and assets should not be recognised unless they can be measured reliably and it is probable that economic benefits will be received.

**137**

An **irrecoverable debt** would be recognised when information comes to light to suggest that a customer is unwilling or unable to pay their debt in full, or even at all

An **allowance for receivables** would be recognised when there is some doubt as to whether some of the entity's receivables may fail to pay their debts in full.

**138**

**Step 1 – Reinstate the debt**

| Debit | Receivables |
|-------|-------------|
| Credit | Irrecoverable debts |

**Step 2 – Recognise the payment**

| Debit | Bank |
|-------|------|
| Credit | Receivables |

**139**

| Debit | Irrecoverable debt expense | $1,750 |
|-------|----------------------------|--------|
| Credit | Allowance for receivables | $1,750 |

**140**

Accounting for irrecoverable debts and allowances for receivables represents an application of the **prudence** concept. Trade receivables, as an asset in the statement of financial position should not be overstated.

**141**

The carry forward of unused inventory is an application of the **matching** concept. This is an extension of the accruals concept.

**142**

**Opening inventory brought forward from the previous year:**

| Debit | Cost of sales |
|-------|---------------|
| Credit | Inventory asset |

**Closing inventory unused at the end of the accounting period:**

| Debit | Inventory asset |
|-------|-----------------|
| Credit | Cost of sales |

**143  D, E and F**

In accordance with IAS 2 costs included within the cost of inventory include all costs incurred in bringing the inventories to their present location and condition, including the cost of purchase and conversion. The conversion costs would include only direct production costs.

D is a non-production cost

E and F are both post conversion.

**144**

| FIFO | The cost of the closing inventory is the cost of the most recent purchases of inventory. |
|------|------------------------------------------------------------------------------------------|
| Unit cost | Used when items of inventory are individually distinguishable and of high value. |
| LIFO | The cost of closing inventory is the cost of the oldest remaining items purchased. |
| AVCO | This method is used when the average cost can be calculated on a periodic and continuous basis. |

**145**

**Periodic** weighted average cost is when an average cost per unit is calculated based upon the cost of the opening inventory plus the cost of all purchases made during the accounting period.

**Continuous** weighted average cost is when an updated average cost per unit is calculated following each purchase of goods. The cost of any subsequent sales are then accounted for at that weighted average cost per unit.

**146  $1,250**

| Date | Transaction | Units | $ per unit | Total $ | Issues | Inventory |
|------|-------------|-------|-----------|---------|--------|-----------|
| 1st January | Opening inventory | 100 | $4.00 per unit | $400 | | |
| 3rd January | Purchased | 120 units | $4.50 per unit | $540 | | |
| 4th January | Purchased | 200 units | $5.00 per unit | $1,000 | | |
| 6th January | Sold | 280 units | $7.00 per unit | $1,960 | 100 @ 4.00 = $400<br>120 @ $4.50 = $540<br>60 @ $5.00 = $300<br>Total = $1,240 | 140 @ $5.00 = $700 |
| 7th January | Purchased | 100 units | $5.50 per unit | $550 | | 140 @ $5.00 = $700<br>100 @ $5.50 = $550<br>Total = $1,250 |

**147  $1,150**

Periodic average = (100 x $4.00) + (120 x $4.50) + (200 x $5.00) + (100 x $5.50)/ (100 + 120 + 200 + 100) = $4.79 per unit.

Closing inventory = 100 + 120 + 200 − 280 + 100 = 240 units

Closing inventory valuation = 240 units x $4.79 = $1,150

**148  $1,195**

| Date | Transaction | Units | $ per unit | Total $ | Average per unit | Issue | Closing Inv |
|------|-------------|-------|-----------|---------|------------------|-------|-------------|
| 1st January | Opening inventory | 100 | $4.00 per unit | $400 | $4.00 | | |
| 3rd January | Purchased | 120 units | $4.50 per unit | $540 | $4.72 | | |
| 4th January | Purchased | 200 units | $5.00 per unit | $1,000 | $4.62 | | |
| 6th January | Sold | 280 units | $7.00 per unit | $1,960 | | 280 @ $4.62 = $1,294 | 140 @ $4.62 = $646 |
| 7th January | Purchased | 100 units | $5.50 per unit | $550 | $4.98 | | 240 @ 4.98 = $1,195 |

**149  A**

In time of rising prices FIFO will always give a higher profit as it removes the older items from inventory first leaving closing inventory with the higher cost inventory remaining. The higher figure for closing inventory will give a reduced cost of sale and result in a higher profit overall.

**150  $1,825**

| Date | Transaction | Units | $ per unit | Closing Inv $ |
|---|---|---|---|---|
| 1st January | Opening inventory | 20 | $15 | $300 |
| 5th January | Purchased | 50 units | $17.50 | 20 @ $15 = $300<br>+ 50 @ $17.50 = $875<br>Total = $1,175 |
| 14th January | Purchased | 80 units | $18 per unit | 20 @ $15 = $300<br>+ 50 @ $17.50 = $875<br>+ 80 @ $18 = $1,440<br>Total = $2,615 |
| 16th January | Sold | 100 units | $25 per unit | 50 @ $18 = $900 |
| 27th January | Purchased | 50 units | $18.50 per unit | 50 @ $18 = $900<br>+ 50 @ $18.50 = $925<br>total = $1,825 |

**151  $1,715**

| | |
|---|---|
| Opening inventory | $300 |
| +  purchases ($875 + $1,440 + $925) | $3,240 |
| −  Closing inventory | ($1,825) |
| Cost of goods sold | $1,715 |

## PREPARE MANUFACTURING ACCOUNTS

### 152  $294,000

Cost of goods manufactured is found as follows:

|  | $ |
|---|---|
| Opening inventories of raw materials | 20,000 |
| Purchases of raw materials | 100,000 |
| Less: Closing inventories of raw materials | (22,000) |
|  | 98,000 |
| Direct wages | 80,000 |
| Prime cost | 178,000 |
| Production overheads | 120,000 |
|  | 298,000 |
| Less: Increase in work-in-progress | (4,000) |
| Cost of goods manufactured | 294,000 |

### 153  D

A decrease in work-in-progress means fewer goods are partly complete, thus the value of completed goods will be higher.

### 154  C

Royalties paid on production are a direct expense and are therefore part of prime cost.

### 155  D

The prime cost of goods manufactured in the total of direct factory costs.

### 156  B

The cost of an extension to a factory is a capital expenditure and would be shown as an asset in the statement of financial position.

# PREPARE FINANCIAL STATEMENTS FOR A SINGLE ENTITY

**157  C**

Receivables are an asset, and so part of the statement of financial position.

**158  B**

Equity share capital is increased and share premium is reduced when a bonus issue is made.

**159  C**

Non-current assets are included in the statement of financial position.

**160  B**

Cost of goods sold is calculated as opening inventory + purchases – closing inventory.  Sales are not included in the calculation.

**161  A**

|  | $ | $ |
|---|---|---|
| Sales | | 5,000 |
| Less Cost of Sales | | |
| Opening inventories | 400 | |
| + Purchases | 3,000 | |
| – Closing inventories | (2,000) | (1,400) |
| Gross Profit | | 3,600 |

**162  B**

|  | $ |
|---|---|
| Gross Profit | 4,300 |
| + Rent received | 200 |
| – Rent paid | (1,000) |
| – Interest paid | (300) |
| Net Profit | 3,200 |

**163  C**

|  | $ |
|---|---|
| Increase in inventories = Increase in working capital | 500 |
| Decrease in bank = Decrease in working capital | (800) |
| Increase in payable = Decrease in working capital | (2,400) |
| Overall decrease in working capital | (2,700) |

**164  D**

Working backwards often confuses candidates. Try drawing up a short example of a statement of profit or loss using simple figures of your own, to prove or disprove the options given – e.g.

|  | $ | $ |
|---|---|---|
| Sales |  | 20,000 |
| Inventories at 31.12.2000 | 2,000 |  |
| Add: Purchases during 2001 | 8,000 |  |
|  | 10,000 |  |
| Less: Inventories at 31.12.2001 | (1,000) |  |
| Cost of goods sold |  | (9,000) |
| Gross profit |  | 11,000 |
| Less: expenses |  | 4,000 |
| Profit for the period |  | 7,000 |

Make all the figures different or you will make mistakes.

You can now see the options A, B and C will not give the correct answer.

**165  B**

Working capital is the total of current assets less current liabilities.

**166  A**

|  | $ |
|---|---|
| Sales | 24,000 |
| COS (bal fig 2) | (9,600) |
| Gross profit (bal fig 1) | 14,400 |
| Indirect expenses | (12,000) |
| Profit for the period (10% × 24,000) | 2,400 |

**167  A**

Revenue reserves can be distributed as dividends, so B is incorrect. Revenue reserves are not set aside to replace revenue items; they could be set aside for a specific purpose but this is only one use of revenue reserves

**168  D**

Dividends proposed are not shown in the statement of changes in equity. Directors' and auditors' fees are normal business expenses and appear in the statement of profit or loss and other comprehensive income.

**169  C**

Total comprehensive income includes the profit for the year as well as any unrealised gains or losses such as a revaluation surplus in the year.

**170  A**

This item is included in the statement of profit or loss for the year.

**171  D**

A reserve is a component of equity. Repayment of a loan is a reduction in liabilities.

**172  B**

The allowance for receivables is technically a liability and not a reserve; it would be shown on the statement of financial position netted off against receivables within current assets.

**173  C**

Dividends paid would be shown on the statement of cash flows, not dividends declared or proposed.  Dividends paid are part of financing activities.

**174  D**

Share premium is a capital reserve created when shares are issued at a price above their nominal value.

**175  D**

A statement of cash flows shows the inflows and outflows of cash for an entity not just for operating activities but also relating to investing activities and financing activities.

**176  C**

Revenue reserves are the retained earnings of an entity and would be increased only with option C. A would increase capital reserves, B would decrease revenue reserves and increase general reserves and D would increase the assets.

**177  $289,100**

Purchases can be found by constructing a control account:

|  | $ |  | $ |
|---|---|---|---|
| Cash paid | 271,150 | Opening payables | 71,300 |
| Discount received | 6,600 | **Purchases ($360,400 – $71,300)** | **289,100** |
| Goods returned | 13,750 |  |  |
| Closing payables | 68,900 |  |  |
|  | 360,400 |  | 360,400 |

**178  $237,000**

Sales can be found by constructing a sales control account:

|  | $ |  | $ |
|---|---|---|---|
| Receivables at 1.1.03 | 30,000 | Receipts less cash sales | 240,000 |
| **Sales ($267,000 – $30,000)** | **237,000** | Receivables at 31.12.03 | 27,000 |
|  | 267,000 |  | 267,000 |

**179  A**

The cost of goods withdrawn from the business by the owner is credited against the cost of purchases to ensure that purchases consist only of goods purchased for resale.

**180  D**

Transfers between revenue reserves, as mentioned in A and B, have no effect on the overall total of revenue reserves; issuing shares at a premium increases capital reserves; the paying of dividends must be from revenue reserves, so these will decrease.

# ANALYSIS OF FINANCIAL STATEMENTS

## IDENTIFY INFORMATION PROVIDED BY ACCOUNTING RATIOS

**181**

If an entity revalues its land and buildings the value of the capital employed will **increase**.

If an entity has property, plant and equipment which are coming to the end of their expected useful lives, this will result in an **increase** to ROCE.

If an entity invests in new property, plant and equipment, this will **decrease** ROCE in the short term.

**182**

| | |
|---|---|
| Sales revenue over the years has remained stable, but costs have increased. | decrease |
| Sales revenue and costs have both decreased but costs by a greater proportion. | increase |
| There was a change in the sales mix which resulted in a higher proportion of more profitable products being sold in the current year. | increase |
| The business won new trade discounts with key suppliers. | increase |

**183**

| Operating a JIT inventory system. | decrease |
|---|---|
| Stock-piling inventory in preparation for a new sales drive. | increase |
| Increasing sales in the year. | no impact |
| Negotiating new contracts with suppliers which include increased discounts. | no impact |

## CALCULATE BASIC ACCOUNTING RATIOS

**184  $500**

|  |  | $ |  |
|---|---|---|---|
| Selling price (SP) | 140 | 700 |  |
| Cost of sales (COS) | 100 | 500 | 700 × 100/140 |
|  |  | ——— |  |
| Gross profit | 40 | ??? |  |
|  |  | ——— |  |

**185  7.5 times**

Rate of inventories turnover is found by dividing cost of goods sold by average inventory. Average inventory is:

$$\left( \frac{24{,}000 + 20{,}000}{2} \right) = \$22{,}000$$

$$\text{Inventory turnover} = \frac{\text{Cost of sales}}{\text{Average inventory}}$$

|  | $ |
|---|---|
| Opening inventory | 24,000 |
| Purchases | 160,000 |
|  | ——— |
|  | 184,000 |
| Less: Closing inventory | (20,000) |
|  | ——— |
| Cost of goods sold | 164,000 |
|  | ——— |

Rate of inventory turnover is therefore 164,000/22,000 = 7.5 times

**186  D**

You need only know the correct formula here.

**187  A**

The gearing ratio is the proportion of long-term loans to shareholders' funds, thus it follows that if a decrease in long-term loans is less than a decrease in the shareholders' funds, the gearing ratio will rise.

**188**

The current ratio is current assets: current liabilities, that is 5,800:2,200 = 2.6:1.

The quick ratio is current assets minus inventory: current liabilities, that is 2,000:2,200 = 0.9:1.

**189  D**

|  | $ |
|---|---|
| Opening inventories | 9,075 |
| Add: Purchases | 36,325 |
|  | 45,400 |
| Less: Closing inventories | (4,500) |
| Cost of sales (i.e. 70% of sales revenue) | 40,900 |

|  | % |  |
|---|---|---|
| Sales revenue | 100 |  |
| Cost of sales | 70 |  |
| Gross profit | 30 | $17,529 (i.e. 30/70 × $40,900) |

**190  49 DAYS**

44,000/324,500 × 365 days = 49 days

Average inventories/COS × 365

Average inventories = (50,000 + 38,000)/2 = 44,000

**191  51 DAYS**

60,000/430,000 × 365 days = 51 days

Trade receivables/Sales × 365

**192  47 DAYS**

40,000/312,500 × 365 days = 47 days

Trade payables/Purchases × 365

**193  1.93:1**

108,000/56,000 = 1.93:1

Current assets: Current liabilities

Current assets = Trade receivables 60,000 + Prepayments 4,000 + Cash in hand 6,000 + Closing inventories 38,000 = 108,000

Current liabilities = Bank overdraft 8,000 + Trade payables 40,000 + Accruals 3,000 + Declared dividends 5,000 = 56,000

**194  1.25:1**

(108,000 – 38,000)/56,000 = 1.25:1

(Current assets – Inventories) : Current liabilities

Current assets and liabilities as above

**195  53 DAYS**

Cash cycle = Inventories days + Receivables days – Payables days = 49 + 51-47 (as per answers above) = 53 days

**196  $80,000**

$32,000/0.4 = $80,000

Current ratio is 1.4:1 and

Current assets – Current liabilities = 32,000

If Current liabilities are A then Current assets are 1.4A

1.4A – A = 32,000; 0.4A = 32,000

Hence A = 32,000/0.4 = Current liabilities

**197  $40,000**

Current liabilities = $80,000; Current assets = $80,000 × 1.4 = $112,000

Quick assets = $80,000 × 0.9 = $72,000

Therefore, inventories will be the difference between current assets and quick assets ($112,000 – 72,000) = $40,000

**198  $468,000**

Cost of sales = $40,000 × 8.775 = $351,000; Gross profit is 25% of sales

Therefore, sales equals to $351,000/0.75 = $468,000

**199  $18,000**

Closing receivables = $468,000 × 6/52 = $54,000

Current assets = $112,000 (see answer 180)

Closing inventories = $40,000 (see answer 180)

Bank balance = $112,000 – $54,000 – $40,000 = $18,000

**200  A**

Capital employed is increased by making a profit, or by adding more capital. Writing off irrecoverable debt would reduce profit; transactions such as C and D merely adjust the split of assets and liabilities but do not add anything overall.

# Section 3

# PRACTICE ASSESSMENT QUESTIONS

1   **Which one of the following items should be classified as capital expenditure?**

   A   Repairs to motor vans

   B   Depreciation of machinery

   C   Extension of premises

   D   Purchase of motor vans for resale

2   **Match the following users with their principal information requirements:**

| | Users | | Requirements |
|---|---|---|---|
| 1 | The public | A | The ability of the company to continue, and to pay pensions in the future |
| 2 | The government | B | The use of information for taking operational decisions in running the company |
| 3 | Employees | C | The policies of a company and how those policies affect the community, for example health and safety |
| 4 | Internal users | D | The performance and financial position of a company and its ability to pay dividends |
| 5 | Shareholders | E | The ability of a company to pay taxes, and administer other taxes, for example value-added tax |

3   **The form and content of management accounts used by an entity are specified by**

   A   company law

   B   company law and international accounting standards

   C   the shareholders

   D   directors

4   **The accounting convention that, in times of rising prices, tends to understate asset values and overstate profits, is the**

   A   going concern convention

   B   prudence convention

   C   realisation convention

   D   historical cost convention

5    **Using the available drag and drop options below complete the following statement.**

Recording the purchase of computer stationery by debiting the computer equipment account would result in _____ of profit and _____ of non-current assets.

Available options          an overstatement/an understatement/no change

(each option can be used more than once)

6    **What does 'Limited' mean in an entity's name e.g.' ABC Limited'?**

A    A company's liability is limited to the total amount of its authorised share capital

B    A company's liability is limited to the total amount of its issued share capital

C    The members' liability is limited to the total amount paid or payable on the shares held by them

D    The members' liability is limited to the nominal value of the shares held by them

7    **Drag and drop the correct option from the list provided to complete the following statement.**

The core objective of accounting is _____.

Options available:        to provide financial information to the users of such information/to maintain records of assets and liabilities/ to keep a record of transactions/to fulfil statutory requirements

8    **Which three of the following items are qualitative characteristics of financial statements in accordance with the IASB's Conceptual Framework for Financial Reporting?**

A    Relevance

B    Comparability

C    Profitability

D    Understandability

E    Accountability

9    Sharon started a business on 1 January 20X1 with $30,000 capital. During the year 20X1 she withdrew $15,000 from the business and paid in a gift of $9,000 from her uncle. At 31 December 20X1 the business's net assets were valued at $54,000.

**Calculate the business profit for the year.**

$....................

10   An imprest system is designed to help reconcile the cash book with the bank statement.

**Is this statement true or false?**

True/false

11      The following information is relates to PQR's receivables:

|  | $ |
|---|---|
| Balance b/f at 1 January 20X3 | 166,200 |
| Allowance for receivables at 1 January 20X3 | 13,320 |
| Increase in provision during 20X3 | 1,440 |
| Discount allowed in year | 47,280 |
| Sales in year | 1,460,760 |
| Contra purchase ledger in year | 106,800 |
| Receipts from customers in year | 1,370,400 |

What was the balance carried forward at 31 December 20X3 on PQR's sales ledger control account?

$ _____

12      JOB purchased goods on credit from SAD for $24,000.

Using the drop down lists provided in the table below identify the correct accounting entries to record this transaction.

| Debit/Credit | Account |
|---|---|
| Debit | Purchases/Receivables/Payables/Cash/Sales |
| Credit | Purchases/Receivables/Payables/Cash/Sales |

13      ALP owed $60 to trade payables at 1 July 20X4 and $90 at 30 June 20X5. Purchases on credit amounted to $3,000 during the year and suppliers allowed a total of $150 cash discount.

How much cash was paid to suppliers during the year?

$....................

14      Red operates the imprest system for petty cash. At 1 March there was a float of $200, but it was decided to increase this to $250 at the 31 March. During March, the petty cashier received $40 from a member of staff who had claimed excessive expenses in a previous month. The cashier then paid $75 for drinks and biscuits, $72 for stationery and $40 for window cleaning.

How much was withdrawn from the bank account for petty cash at the end of March?

$...................

15      Assuming that it reconciles with the cash book, how would a balance marked 'Cr' on a business's bank statement be classified in an entity's statement of financial position?

A       Current asset

B       Current liability

C       Non-current asset

D       Non-current liability

**16**     A purchases day book total $7,390 had been entered in the control account as $7,930.

**What will be the impact when the required correction is made?**

|   | Control account | List of balances |
|---|---|---|
| A | Debit $540 | No effect |
| B | Debit $540 | Decrease total by $540 |
| C | Credit $540 | No effect |
| D | Debit $1,080 | No effect |

**17**     At 31 December 20X4, an entity's cash book had a debit balance of $8,400. The bank statement at that date had an overdrawn balance of $2,520.

**Which one of the following timing differences could account for the discrepancy?**

A     Cheques drawn but not yet presented amounted to $5,880

B     Cheques received but not yet cleared amounted to $5,880

C     Cheques drawn but not yet presented amounted to $10,920

D     Cheques received but not yet cleared amounted to $10,920

**18**     **Which of the following errors would not cause there to be a difference in the trial balance?**

A     incomplete double entry

B     addition error

C     transaction not recorded at all

D     transposition error in the debit entry

**19**     **State whether each of the following two statements are true or false**

A     An integrated report contains only historical financial information

True/False

B     An integrated report is the same thing as the notes to the financial statements

True/False

**20**     GRE paid $3,600 insurance during the year to 31 March 20X1.

As at 1 April 20X0 GRE had overpaid $1,200, and the correct charge in the statement of profit or loss for year to 31 March 20X1 was $3,900.

**What was the amount of the prepayment at 31 March 20X1?**

$....................

**21**   Drag and drop the correct option from the list provided to complete the following statement.

Businesses charge depreciation on non-current assets in order to _____.

Options available:

ensure that sufficient funds are available to replace the assets/

spread the cost of the assets over their estimated useful life/

comply with the prudence convention/

reduce profits and dividends

**22**   An entity purchased a car for $60,000 on 1 July 20X3 and expected it to have a useful life of 5 years. It depreciated the car using 50% reducing balance and sold it on 30 June 20X6 for $30,000.

**What was the profit on disposal?**

$....................

**23**   GRA has the following balances in its trial balance at 31 December 20X3.

|  | $ |
|---|---|
| Total receivables | 420,000 |
| Irrecoverable debts written off (no previous allowance) | 3,000 |
| Allowance for receivables at 1 January 20X3 | 30,000 |

GRA wishes to carry forward an allowance for receivables equal to 10% of total receivables.

**What is the total effect of the above on the statement of profit or loss for the year ended 31 December 20X3?**

A      A charge of $14,700

B      A credit of $14,700

C      A charge of $15,000

D      A credit of $15,000

**24**   **Under which heading should debentures be classified in an entity's statement of financial position?**

A      Equity

B      Current assets

C      Current liabilities

D      Non-current liabilities

**25**   KIR sells three products X, Y and Z. At KIR's reporting date the inventories held were as follows:

|   | Cost | Selling price |
|---|------|---------------|
|   | $ | $ |
| X | 3,600 | 4,500 |
| Y | 18,600 | 18,300 |
| Z | 2,760 | 2,790 |

At sale a 5% commission is payable by KIR to its agent.

**What was the total value these inventories in KIR's financial statements?**

A   $23,636

B   $24,282

C   $24,960

D   $25,635

**26**   DEF sold goods with a list price of $1,000 to Khan which was subject to trade discount of 5% and early settlement discount of 4% if the invoice was paid within 7 days. The normal credit period available to credit customers is 30 days from invoice date. At the point of sale, Khan was not expected to take advantage of early settlement terms offered. Khan subsequently paid within 7 days.

**What accounting entries should be made by DEF to record settlement of the amount due?**

A   Debit Cash $950, Debit Revenue $50 and Credit Trade receivables $1,000

B   Debit Cash $950, Credit Revenue $38 and Credit Trade receivables $912

C   Debit Cash $912, Debit Revenue $38 and Credit Trade receivables $950

D   Debit Cash $912, and Credit Trade receivables $912

**27**   An entity sold goods with a net value of $200,000 and made purchases with a gross value of $162,000. All transactions were subject to sales tax at the rate of 20%.

**What was the balance on the sales tax account based upon this information?**

A   $933

B   $6,333

C   $7,600

D   $13,000

**28**   HEO sold a motor van which it had purchased three years ago at a cost of $24,000 and which it depreciated each year at 50% using the reducing balance method.

HEO traded this van in for a new vehicle which had a cost of $36,000, and paid the supplying garage $34,400 by cheque.

**Using the number entry field and the drop down text below - what was the profit or loss on the sale of the old van?**

$.................... profit/loss

**29** EUR owns property which it lets to tenants, MED and ORE. EUR is currently preparing its financial statements for the year ended 31 December 20X6. The following information is available:

|  | Medea | Orestes |
|---|---|---|
|  | $ | $ |
| Rent paid in advance 31.12.X5 | 1,000 |  |
| Rent owed 31.12.X5 |  | 1,400 |
| Rent paid during year | 4,000 | 5,000 |
| Rent paid in advance at 31.12.X6 |  | 500 |
| Rent owed at 31.12.X6 | 200 |  |

**What figure for rental income will appear in EUR's statement of profit or loss for the year ended 31 December 20X6?**

A $8,300

B $8,900

C $9,100

D $9,700

**30** BOW's accounting year end is 31 December. For various reasons, inventories could not be counted as at 31 December 20X5 until 6 January 20X6. The inventories were counted on 6 January 20X6 and, at that date, were valued at $445,800. Detailed records were kept of inventories movements between the 31 December 20X5 and the physical inventory count on 6 January 20X6. The following figures (all stated at cost) are available:

|  | $ |
|---|---|
| Sales | 7,500 |
| Purchases | 6,930 |
| Returns inwards | 1,650 |
| Returns outwards | 840 |

**In accordance with IAS 2 *Inventories*, what was BOW's inventory valuation at 31 December 20X5?**

$_____

**31** MRM paid rent of $14,400 for the period 1 January 20X4 to 31 December 20X4. MRM's financial statements prepared for the nine months ended 30 September 20X4 should include which of the following amounts?

A Only a rent expense of $10,800

B A rent expense of $10,800 and a prepayment of $3,600

C A rent expense of $10,800 and accrued revenue of $3,600

D A rent expense of $14,400 with an explanatory note that this is the charge for twelve months

32    ATO purchased a machine for which the supplier's list price was $162,000. ATO paid $117,000 cash and traded in an old machine which had a carrying amount of $72,000. It is ATO's policy to depreciate such machines at the rate of 10% per annum on cost.

What was the carrying amount of the machine after one year?

A    $105,300

B    $145,800

C    $170,100

D    $172,800

33    **Using the drag and drop options available below complete the following statement.**

The difference between a statement of profit or loss and an income and expenditure statement is that_____.

an income and expenditure statement is an alternative international accounting term for a statement of profit or loss

a statement of profit or loss prepared for a business entity and an income and expenditure statement is prepared for a non-profit-making organisation

a statement of profit or loss is prepared on an accruals basis and an income and expenditure account is prepared on a cash flow basis

a statement of profit or loss is prepared for a manufacturing business and an income and expenditure statement is prepared for a non-manufacturing business

34    The following information is given for DEF for the year ended 31 October 20X0:

| | $ |
|---|---|
| Purchase of raw materials | 28,000 |
| Returns inwards | 2,000 |
| Increase in inventories of raw materials | 850 |
| Direct wages | 10,500 |
| Carriage inwards | 1,250 |
| Production overheads | 7,000 |
| Decrease in work-in-progress | 2,500 |

**What was the DEF's factory cost of goods completed?**

$_____

35    **Which one of the following costs should be included in the calculation of prime cost in a manufacturing account?**

A    Cost of transporting raw materials from suppliers premises

B    Wages of factory workers engaged in machine maintenance

C    Depreciation of lorries used for deliveries to customers

D    Cost of indirect production materials

**36**   FRE's inventories on 1 January 20X4 cost $14,300 and its payables were $3,750. During the year, sales amounted to $174,000, earning an average mark-up of 33% on cost. FRE paid $133,650 to suppliers during the year and payables' balances at 31 December 20X4 totalled $4,900. On the same date FRE's shop was burgled and all inventories were stolen.

**What was the cost of the stolen inventories?**

A    $16,300

B    $18,273

C    $30,800

D    $33,100

**37**   The reducing-balance method of depreciating non-current assets is more appropriate than the straight-line method when:

A    there is no expected residual value for the asset

B    the expected life of the asset is not capable of being estimated

C    the asset is expected to be replaced in a short period of time

D    it more accurately reflects the consumption of the asset

**38**   Which of the following items should be classified as revenue expenditure?

A    Drawings of goods for private consumption by the proprietor

B    Petrol for proprietor's wife's private car

C    Purchase of a new word processor

D    Purchase of an ink cartridge for the word processor

**39**   A business entity had opening inventories of $24,000 and closing inventories of $36,000. During the accounting period, it made purchase returns of $10,000. The cost of goods sold was $222,000.

**What was the cost of purchases?**

$ _____

**40**   At 30 June 20X7, TRE had issued share capital of $10,000, consisting of ordinary shares of $0.50 each, a share premium account of $5,000 and retained earnings of $57,000. TRE made a bonus issue of shares of 'one for five' on 30 June 20X7.

**Select from the items available to state the accounting entries required to record this issue of shares along with the value of the transaction.**

|  |  | $ |
|---|---|---|
| Debit: | Cash/Share capital/Share premium | $1,000/$2,000/$4,000 |
| Credit: | Cash/Share capital/Share premium | $1,000/$2,000/$4,000 |

**41** Classify each of the following costs as either an expense or an intangible asset that should be capitalised in accordance with IAS 38 *Intangible Assets.*

| | Expense | Intangible asset |
|---|---|---|
| Employee training costs | | |
| Plant and machinery running costs | | |
| Cost of purchasing a five-year product licence | | |
| Market research costs | | |

**42** CLA paid $20,400 cash for electricity during the year ended 31 December 20X3. At 1 January 20X3 CLA owed $15,000 and at 31 December 20X3 it owed $17,400.

**What charge for electricity should appear in CLA's statement of profit or loss for the year ended 31 December 20X3?**

A $17,400

B $18,000

C $20,400

D $22,800

**43** What action does an entity need to take upon discovery that a major customer has become insolvent? An allowance for this receivable had been made at the end of the previous year.

**The entries required to write off the amount outstanding are:**

A Dr Irrecoverable debts      Cr Receivables

B Dr Receivables      Cr Irrecoverable debts

C Dr Receivables      Cr Allowance for receivables

D Dr Allowance for receivables      Cr Receivables

**44** **Which one of the following statements best defines an expense?**

A An expense is an outflow of economic benefits resulting from a claim by a third party

B An expense is a decrease in assets or increase in liabilities that result in a decreases in equity, other than those relating to distributions to holders of equity claims

C An expense is any outflow of economic benefits in an accounting period

D An expense is an outflow of economic benefits resulting from the purchase of resources in an accounting period

**45** **In which financial statements would you expect to include a loss on disposal of property plant and equipment?** Choose all that apply.

A The statement of cash flows

B The statement of financial position

C The statement of profit or loss and other comprehensive income

D The statement of changes in equity

**46** XYZ's plant and machinery had a carrying value of $450,000 at the year end. Its opening balance was $325,000. During the year, depreciation of $63,000 was charged and an asset with a carrying value of $12,000 was disposed of resulting in a profit on disposal of $3,000.

What it the cash outflow for purchases of plant and machinery in the year?

$...................

**47** CAN returned some goods to a supplier because they were faulty. The original purchase price of these goods was $24,780.

The ledger clerk treated the return correctly on both the payables' ledger control account and the individual payables' account, but debited the purchase returns account with $25,860.

Using the drop downs available in the table below to show the correcting entry that needs to be made.

| Debit/Credit | Account | Amount |
|---|---|---|
| Debit | Purchases returns/Receivables returns/Suspense/Cash/Payables | $1080/$50,640 |
| Credit | Purchases returns/Receivables returns/Suspense/Cash/Payables | $1080/$50,640 |

**48** An entity had the following trading account for the year ending 31 May 2008:

|  | $ | $ |
|---|---|---|
| Sales revenue |  | 90,000 |
| Opening inventory | 8,000 |  |
| Add: Purchases | 53,000 |  |
|  | 61,000 |  |
| Less: Closing inventory | (12,000) |  |
|  |  | (49,000) |
| Gross profit |  | 41,000 |

What was its rate of inventory turnover for the year?

.................. times (to 1 decimal place)

**49** The financial statements of FGH for the years ended 30 September 20X3 and 20X4 respectively included the following:

|  | 20X3 | 20X4 |
|---|---|---|
|  | $ | $ |
| Share capital of $1 each | 40,000 | 46,000 |
| Share premium | 10,000 | 12,000 |
| Retained earnings | 63,000 | 72,500 |

During the year ended 30 September 20X4, loan notes of $8,000 at par were issued.

**What was the net cash inflow or outflow from financing activities during the year ended 30 September 20X4?**

……………… Inflow/outflow (delete which does not apply)

**50** KLN recorded the following transactions in its financial statements for the year ended 31 October 20X6:

- a revaluation surplus of $15,000 on revaluation of property

- depreciation charge of $4,200

- loss on disposal of property, plant and equipment of $3250

**What amount should be included in 'other comprehensive income' within the statement of profit or loss and other comprehensive income for the year ended 31 October 20X6?**

$………………

**51** WXY provided the following information relating to its financial statements for the year ended 28 February 20X5:

|  | $ | $ |
|---|---|---|
| Sales revenue |  | 372,640 |
| Less: Cost of goods sold |  |  |
| Inventories at 1 March 20X4 | 13,750 |  |
| Purchases | 298,957 |  |
| Less: inventory at 28 February 20X5 | ??? |  |
| Gross profit |  | ??? |

Subsequently, WXY identified that the sales revenue figure should have been stated as $372,463 and that sales returns of $2,468 and purchases returns of $4,268 had been omitted form the information above. WXY earns a 20% gross profit margin on sales.

**What was WXY's value of inventories at 28 February 20X5?**

$………………

**52** An entity's cash book had an opening balance in the bank column of $900 credit. 'The following transactions then took place:

- cash sales $2,300 including sales tax of $300

- receipts from customers of $7,200

- payments to payables of $5,000 less 5% cash discount

- dishonoured cheques from customers amounting to $400.

**The closing balance in the bank column of the cash book should be:**

$.................... debit/credit.

**53** Following extraction of a trial balance, INT created a suspense account with a debit balance of $2,250. Upon investigation, the following errors were found:

- the closing balance of the purchase ledger control account had been overcast by $2,100

- the purchase returns daybook had been overcast by $660.

- The list of purchase ledger balances included a debit balance of $400 which had been counted as a credit balance when arriving at the total of the purchase ledger balances

**When these items had been corrected, what was the balance remaining on the suspense account?**

$.................... debit/credit.

**54** **An entity made a profit of $4,000 but its bank balance has fallen by $2,500. This could be due to**

A depreciation of $1,500 and an increase in inventories of $5,000

B depreciation of $3,000 and the repayment of a loan of $3,500

C depreciation of $6,000 and the purchase of new non-current assets for $12,500

D the disposal of a non-current asset for $6,500 less than its carrying amount

**55** JAD received cash from JOS in part-payment of an amount owed.

**Using the drop down menus available in the table below select the correct accounting entries to record the receipt of cash by JAD.**

| Debit | Credit |
|---|---|
| Cash/Sales/Payables/Receivables | Cash/Sales/Payables/Receivables |

**56** **Which THREE of the following statements relating to depreciation are true?**

A    Accounting for depreciation reduces the profit for the year

B    Accounting for depreciation generates cash for the business

C    Not all items of property, plant and equipment are depreciated

D    Accounting for depreciation results in a cash outflow

E    The same method and rate of depreciation should be applied to all items of property, plant and equipment

**57** PQR sold goods with a list price of $4,500 to Singh which was subject to trade discount of 5% and early settlement discount of 4% if the invoice was paid within 7 days. The normal credit period available to credit customers is 30 days from invoice date. At the point of sale, Singh was expected to take advantage of the early settlement terms offered. However, on this occasion, Singh did not pay within 7 days.

**What accounting entries should be made by PQR to record settlement of the amount outstanding?**

A    Debit Cash $4,104, Debit Revenue $396 and Credit Trade receivables $4,500

B    Debit Cash $4,275, Debit Discount received $171 and Credit Trade receivables $4,104

C    Debit Cash $4,275 and Credit Trade receivables $4,275

D    Debit Cash $4,275, Credit Trade receivables $4,104 and Credit Revenue $171

**58** **Using the drag and drop options available, complete the following statement.**

Goodwill is most appropriately classed as _____.

**Available options:**

a current asset/an intangible asset/a fictitious liability/a semi-non-current asset

**59** **Which one of the following is most likely to increase the trade receivables collection period?**

A    Offering credit customers a significant discount for prompt payment within seven days of receipt of the invoice

B    Paying suppliers promptly within seven days of receipt of invoice

C    An increased volume of credit sales in comparison with the previous accounting period

D    Poor application of credit control by an entity

**60** JKL had tangible non-current assets with a carrying amount of $60,000 at 31 May 20X8 and $57,600 at 31 May 20X9. During the year ended 31 May 2019, JKL charged depreciation of $8,500 and disposed of property plant and equipment which had cost $6,000 and on which accumulated depreciation was $2,500.

**What was the cash paid for property, plant and equipment additions during the year ended 31 May 20X9?**

$··················

# Section 4

# ANSWERS TO PRACTICE ASSESSMENT QUESTIONS

1    C

2    1C, 2E, 3A, 4B, 5D

3    D

4    D

5    Recording the purchase of computer stationery by debiting the computer equipment account would result in **an overstatement** of profit and **an overstatement** of non-current assets.

6    C

7    The core objective of accounting is **to provide financial information to the users of such information.**

8    A, B and D

9    **$30,000**

Initial capital – drawings + further capital introduced (legacy) +/– profit/(loss) = Closing capital (net assets)

30,000 – 15,000 + 9,000 +/– profit/(loss) = 54,000

Therefore profit = 54,000 – 30,000 + 15,000 – 9,000 = 30,000

10   **False**

The imprest system helps to control petty cash, not the bank account.

**11    $102,480**

### SLCA

| | | | |
|---|---:|---|---:|
| Bal b/f | 166,200 | Revenue (Discount allowed) | 47,280 |
| Sales | 1,460,760 | Contra purchase ledger | 106,800 |
| | | Receipts from receivables | 1,370,400 |
| | | Bal c/f (bal fig) | 102,480 |
| | 1,626,960 | | 1,626,960 |

**12**

| Debit/Credit | Account |
|---|---|
| Debit | Purchases |
| Credit | Payables |

**13    $2,820**

### Payables

| | $ | | $ |
|---|---:|---|---:|
| Discount received | 150 | Bal b/d | 60 |
| Cash (bal. fig.) | 2,820 | Purchases | 3,000 |
| Bal c/d | 90 | | |
| | 3,060 | | 3,060 |

**14    $197**

| | $ |
|---|---:|
| Opening petty cash float | 200 |
| Received from member of staff | 40 |
| Paid out in expenses | |
| (75 + 72 + 40) | (187) |
| | 53 |
| From bank account (bal fig) | 197 |
| Required closing cash float | 250 |

**15    A**

**16    A**

**17    D**

Cheques received were lodged into the bank but were not yet cleared.

**18    C**

**19    BOTH STATEMENTS ARE FALSE**

**20    $900**

<table>
<tr><td colspan="4" align="center">**Insurance**</td></tr>
<tr><td></td><td>$</td><td></td><td>$</td></tr>
<tr><td>Bal b/d</td><td>1,200</td><td>Statement of profit or loss</td><td>3,900</td></tr>
<tr><td>Cash</td><td>3,600</td><td>Bal c/d</td><td>900</td></tr>
<tr><td></td><td>4,800</td><td></td><td>4,800</td></tr>
</table>

**21**    Businesses charge depreciation on non-current assets in order to **spread the cost of the assets over their estimated useful life.**

**22    $22,500**

| | $ |
|---|---|
| Cost | 60,000 |
| Depreciation year 1: $60,000 × 50% | (30,000) |
| | 30,000 |
| Depreciation year 2: $30,000 × 50% | (15,000) |
| | 15,000 |
| Depreciation year 3: $7,500 × 50% | (7,500) |
| | 7,500 |

<table>
<tr><td colspan="4" align="center">**Non-current asset disposal account**</td></tr>
<tr><td></td><td>$</td><td></td><td>$</td></tr>
<tr><td>Cost (original cost always)</td><td>60,000</td><td>Accumulated depreciation</td><td>52,500</td></tr>
<tr><td>SP&L (balancing figure)</td><td>22,500</td><td>Sale proceeds</td><td>30,000</td></tr>
<tr><td></td><td>82,500</td><td></td><td>82,500</td></tr>
</table>

**23    C**

### Allowance for receivables

|  | $ |  | $ |
|---|---|---|---|
| Bal c/d (10% × 420,000) | 42,000 | Bal b/d | 30,000 |
|  |  | Irrec. debts a/c | 12,000 |
|  | 42,000 |  | 42,000 |

### Irrecoverable debts expense

|  | $ |  | $ |
|---|---|---|---|
| Allowance for receivables | 12,000 | Statement of profit or loss | 15,000 |
| Irrec. debts written off | 3,000 |  |  |
|  | 15,000 |  | 15,000 |

**Note:** Since the irrecoverable debt write off appears in the trial balance, receivables must already have been adjusted.

**24    D**

A debenture is a long-term loan. It should be classified as a non-current liability.

**25    A**

In accordance with IAS 2 *Inventories*, inventories are valued at lower of cost and net realisable value (costs to be incurred in selling inventories are deducted from selling price in computing NRV)

|  | Cost | Price less commission | Lower of cost and NRV |
|---|---|---|---|
| A | 3,600 | 4,275 | 3,600 |
| B | 18,600 | 17,385 | 17,385 |
| C | 2,760 | 2,651 | 2,651 |
|  |  |  | 23,636 |

Here each item A, B and C are considered separately and not collectively as a group.

**26    C**

Trade discount is always deducted when calculating the amount invoiced by the seller. In addition, as Khan was not expected to take account of the early settlement discount terms, the amount of revenue receivable is calculated after deduction of trade discount only at $950 ($1000 × 95%).

When Khan subsequently pays early to be eligible for the discount, the accounting entries should reflect that fact and record settlement of the amount outstanding and also reduced revenue.

Debit Cash $912 ($950 × 96%), Debit Revenue $38 ($950 × 4%), and Credit Trade receivables $950.

**27    D**

|  | $ |
|---|---|
| Output sales tax on sales (20% × $200,000) | 40,000 |
| Input sales tax on purchases (20/120 × $162,000) | (27,000) |
|  | 13,000 |

**28    $1,400 LOSS**

**Non-current asset disposal account**

| | | | |
|---|---|---|---|
| Cost | 24,000 | Accumulated depreciation | 21,000 |
| Paid | 34,400 | New van | 36,000 |
| | | SP&L | 1,400 |
| | 58,400 | | 58,400 |

12,000 + 6,000 + 3,000 = 21,000

| | |
|---|---|
| Cost | 24,000 |
| Depreciation 50% | (12,000) |
| | 12,000 |
| Depreciation 50% | (6,000) |
| | 6,000 |
| Depreciation 50% | (3,000) |

**29 A**

**Rent receivable account**

| | $ | | $ |
|---|---|---|---|
| Bal b/d (Orsetes) | 1,400 | Bal b/d (Medea) | 1,000 |
| SP&L (balancing figure) | 8,300 | Recorded in year (4,000 + 5,000) | 9,000 |
| Bal c/d (Orestes) | 500 | Bal c/d (Medea) | 200 |
| | 10,200 | | 10,200 |
| Bal b/d (Medea) | 200 | Bal b/d (Orestes) | 500 |

**30 $445,560**

445,800 + 7,500 − 6,930 − 1,650 + 840 = $445,560

**31 B**

14,400 × 9/12 = $10,800 Rent expense and 14,400 − 10,800 = $3,600 Prepayment

**32 B**

$162,000 × 90% = $145,800

The carrying amount of $72,000 of the trade-in old machine is irrelevant. The trade-in value agreed is evidently $45,000, which is the difference between the supplier's price and the cash paid.

**33** The difference between a statement of profit or loss and an income and expenditure statement is that **a statement of profit or loss prepared for a business entity and an income and expenditure statement is prepared for a non-profit-making organisation.**

**34 $48,400**

| | $ |
|---|---|
| Purchase of raw material | 28,000 |
| Carriage inwards | 1,250 |
| Increase in inventories | (850) |
| Cost of material consumed | 28,400 |
| Direct wages | 10,500 |
| Prime cost | 38,900 |
| Production overheads | 7,000 |
| Decrease in work-in-progress | 2,500 |
| Production cost | 48,400 |

**35  A**

The cost of transporting raw materials forms part of the direct material costs.

**36  B**

|  | $ |  |
|---|---|---|
| Sales | 174,000 |  |
| Opening inventories | 14,300 |  |
| Purchases (see below) | 134,800 |  |
|  | 149,100 |  |
| Less: Closing inventories | $18,273 | = Balancing figure |
| Cost of sales (see below) | 130,827 |  |

**PLCA**

|  | $ |  | $ |
|---|---|---|---|
| Paid payables | 133,650 | Bal b/f | 3,750 |
| Bal c/d | 4,900 | Purchases (balancing figure) | 134,800 |
|  | 138,550 |  | 138,550 |

|  | % |  | $ |
|---|---|---|---|
| Balance | 133% | Sales | 174,000 |
| Mark-up | 100% | (Cost of sales) | ??? |
| Given | 33% | Gross profit |  |

Therefore, cost of sales = $174,000 × 100/133 = $130,827

**37  D**

**38  D**

**39  $244,000**

Reconstruction of cost of goods sold to establish the purchases figure:

|  | $ | $ |
|---|---|---|
| Opening inventories |  | 24,000 |
| Add: Purchases | 244,000* |  |
| Less: Returns | (10,000) | 234,000 |
| Closing inventories |  | (36,000) |
| Cost of goods sold |  | 222,000 |

*Found by difference

**40**

|  |  | $ |
|---|---|---|
| Debit: | Share premium | 2,000 |
| Credit: | Share capital | 2,000 |

Shares issued = $10,000 × 2 = 20,000 shares in issue /5 = 4,000 bonus shares at $0.5 each

**41**

|  | Expense | Intangible asset |
|---|---|---|
| Employee training costs | Yes | No |
| Plant and machinery running costs | Yes | No |
| Cost of purchasing a five-year product licence | No | Yes |
| Market research costs | Yes | No |

**42 D**

**Electricity**

| | $ | | $ |
|---|---|---|---|
| Cash paid | 20,400 | Bal b/f | 15,000 |
| Bal c/d | 17,400 | SP&L | 22,800 |
| | 37,800 | | 37,800 |

**43 A**

D is wrong because the allowance for receivables is only adjusted at the end of each accounting period.

**44 B**

All other suggested answers include only part of the definition of an expense – they are not precise enough or comprehensive enough.

**45 A and C**

A loss on disposal of plant and equipment will be included in the statement of cash flows as an adjustment to profit before tax in arriving at net cash flows from operating activities and it will also be included in the statement of profit or loss and other comprehensive income.

**46   $200,000**

**Plant & machinery**

| | $000 | | $000 |
|---|---|---|---|
| Bal b/f | 325 | Depreciation | 63 |
| | | Disposal | 12 |
| Additions | 200 | Bal c/f | 450 |
| (bal fig = cash paid) | | | |
| | ——— | | ——— |
| | 525 | | 525 |
| | ——— | | ——— |

**47**

| Debit/Credit | Account | Amount |
|---|---|---|
| Debit | Suspense | $50,640 |
| Credit | Purchases returns | $50,640 |

Correct entry was to credit purchases returns account with $24,780. To correct, credit purchases returns with $24,780 + $25,860. Suspense account is to be debited, as the original entry will have created a suspense account balance by putting the accounts out of balance.

**48   4.9 times**

Rate of inventory turnover is found by dividing cost of goods sold by average inventory.

Average inventory = (8,000 + 12,000)/2 = $10,000

Cost of goods sold is $49,000

Rate of inventory turnover is therefore 49,000/10,000 = 4.9 times

**49   $16,000 INFLOW**

| | 20X3 | 20X4 |
|---|---|---|
| | $ | $ |
| Proceeds of share issue | ($6,000 + $2,000) | 8,000 |
| Issue of loan notes | | 8,000 |
| | | ——— |
| | | 16,000 |
| | | ——— |

**50**   **$15,000**

Only the revaluation surplus is included on 'other comprehensive income'. All other items are accounted for in the statement of profit or loss.

**51**   **$12,443**

|  | $ | $ |
|---|---|---|
| Sales revenue ($372,463 - $2,468) |  | 369,995 |
| Less: Cost of goods sold |  |  |
| Inventories at 1 March 20X4 | 13,750 |  |
| Purchases ($298,957 - $4,268) | 294,689 |  |
| Less: inventory at 28 February 20X5 | (12,443) |  |
| (80% × $369,995) |  | 295,996 |
| Gross profit (20% × $369,995) |  | 73,999 |

**52**   **$3,450 debit**

The calculation is as follows:

|  | $ |
|---|---|
| Opening over draft | (900) |
| Add cash sales, including sales tax | 2,300 |
| Add receipts from customers | 7,200 |
| Less payments after discount | (4,750) |
| Less dishonoured cheques | (400) |
| Closing balance | 3,450 |

**53    $150 DEBIT**

### Suspense account

|  | $ |  | $ |
|---|---|---|---|
| Balance per Trial Balance | 2,250 | Overstated PLCA balance | 2,100 |
|  |  | Balance c/d | 150 |
|  | 2,250 |  | 2,250 |
| Balance b/d | 150 |  |  |

The casting error in the purchase returns daybook affects debit balances and credit balances equally, so will not contribute towards clearing the suspense account balance. The list of purchase ledger balances is not part of the double entry accounting system and therefore will not contribute towards clearing the suspense account balance.  The only error that contributes towards clearance of the suspense account is the casting error on the purchase ledger control account.

This is corrected by the following adjustment:

Debit: PLCA (to reduce the balance on the PLCA to the correct amount) $2,100

Credit: Suspense $2,100

**54    C**

|  | $ |
|---|---|
| Profit | 4,000 |
| Add back depreciation | 6,000 |
| Net cash inflow | 10,000 |
| Purchase of non-current assets | (12,500) |
| Decrease | (2,500) |

**55**

| Debit | Credit |
|---|---|
| **Cash** | **Receivables** |

**56    A, C and D**

Re option C – land is not depreciated as this does not have a finite useful life.  Re option D – accounting for depreciation results in recognition of an expense and an increase in the accumulated depreciation provision – it is not a cash flow. Re option E – different classes of property. Plant and equipment (e.g. buildings, vehicles, and equipment) will be subject to different methods of depreciation (e.g. straight-line or reducing balance) and at different rates to match how they are used in the business.

**57    D**

Trade discount is always deducted when calculating the amount invoiced by the seller. In addition, as Khan is expected to take account of the early settlement discount terms, the amount of revenue receivable is calculated after deduction of both trade discount and early settlement discount, a total of $4,104 ($4,500 × 95% × 96%). When Khan subsequently pays outside the settlement discount period, the full amount of the receivable $4,275 ($4,500 × 95%) is due. The additional cash received in excess of the receivable amount of $171 is therefore accounted for as a cash sale as follows:

Debit Cash $4,275, Credit Trade receivables $4,104 and Credit Revenue $171.

**58**    Goodwill is most appropriately classed **as an intangible asset as per IAS 38** *Intangible Assets***.**

Goodwill arises when more is paid for the net assets of a business than their fair value. Thus, an additional asset is acquired; it is intangible and should be subject to regular impairment reviews to check that the goodwill is not overstated in the statement of financial position.

**59    D**

If a significant discount is offered to credit customers, some will be likely to take advantage of this, and therefore reduce the trade receivables collection period. Any decisions relating to payment of trade payables will not affect the trade receivables collection period. An increase in the volume of credit sales will not, in itself, increase the trade receivables collection period.

**60    $10,600**

**Property, plant and equipment**

|  | $ |  | $ |
|---|---|---|---|
| Bal b/f | 60,000 | Depreciation | 8,500 |
|  |  | Disposal ($6,000-$2,500) | 3,500 |
| Cash paid | 9,600 | Bal c/f | 57,600 |
|  | 69,600 |  | 69,600 |

# Section 5

# REFERENCES

The Board (2019) *IAS 1 Presentation of Financial Statements*. London: IFRS Foundation

The Board (2019) *IAS 2 Inventories*. London: IFRS Foundation.

The Board (2019) *IAS 7 Statement of Cashflows.* London: IFRS Foundation

The Board (2019) *IAS 16 Property, Plant and Equipment*. London: IFRS Foundation.

The Board (2019) *IAS 38 Intangible Assets*. London: IFRS Foundation.

The Board (2019) *The Conceptual Framework for Financial Reporting*. London: IFRS Foundation